WILL
HE GO?

ALSO BY LAWRENCE DOUGLAS

Nonfiction

*The Right Wrong Man: John Demjanjuk and the Last Great
Nazi War Crimes Trial*

*The Memory of Judgment: Making Law and History in the
Trials of the Holocaust*

Fiction

The Vices

The Catastrophist

Satire

Sense and Nonsensibility (with Alexander George)

WILL HE GO?

Trump and the
Looming Election
Meltdown in 2020

LAWRENCE DOUGLAS

TWELVE

NEW YORK BOSTON

Twelve
Hachette Book Group
1290 Avenue of the Americas, New York, NY 10104

twelvebooks.com

twitter.com/twelvebooks

First Edition: May 2020

Twelve is an imprint of Grand Central Publishing. The Twelve name and logo are trademarks of Hachette Book Group, Inc.

The publisher is not responsible for websites (or their content) that are not owned by the publisher.

The Hachette Speakers Bureau provides a wide range of authors for speaking events. To find out more, go to www.hachettespeakersbureau.com or call (866) 376-6591.

Library of Congress Cataloging-in-Publication Data has been applied for.

ISBNs: 978-1-5387-5188-6 (hardcover), 978-1-5387-5187-9 (ebook)

Printed in the United States of America

LSC-C

3 5 7 9 10 8 6 4 2

For my brother Barry,
who teased me in 2016

CONTENTS

INTRODUCTION

On the last day of August 2019, a group of prominent scholars gathered in a conference room in the Bipartisan Policy Center in Washington, D.C. Befitting the center's mission, the scholars represented Democrats and Republicans, progressives and conservatives. What brought them together was a shared expertise in presidential electoral law. That, and a fear that our process for electing the president might be vulnerable to spectacular failure.

To describe the threat facing our system, some of the experts borrowed metaphors from astrophysics. An asteroid is heading straight toward America. Are we equipped to knock it out of the sky? Others spoke in meteorological terms. A Katrina-like storm is gathering off our shores; how strong is our system of levees?

Their sobering answer—prepare for a flood.

For tens of millions of Americans, the 2020 election promises to accomplish what the impeachment proceeding never stood a chance of doing—remove Donald Trump from office. For those who questioned the tactical wisdom of impeaching the president, focusing on 2020 was always the better way to go.

Come Tuesday, November 3, at issue will not be whether Trump committed high crimes or misdemeanors but whether he has earned another term as the nation's chief executive. Republican lawmakers cannot accuse Democrats of trying to defeat the will of the people if the people vote Trump out of the White House.

Of course, there is no guarantee that Trump will be defeated at the polls. But if he is, he will leave the White House not as a martyr of Congress but as a rejected incumbent. Trump survived the judgment of the Senate; he will have no choice but to submit to the verdict of the voters.

That is the hope, anyway.

Some observers, however, have expressed grave doubts about the coming election, including several of the experts gathered last summer in the D.C. conference room. Their concern was not that Trump might win the election, or that he might steal it through disinformation, foreign interference, and voter suppression, real as those concerns are. Their worry was different. What if the election produced an unclear result, one that could be contested? Or what if Trump lost—but refused to acknowledge or accept his defeat?

To believe that beating Trump at the polls provides not only the proper but also the most secure way of removing him from office is to miss the singular menace that this president represents to a basic principle of democratic governance: the peaceful succession of power. If Trump is thoroughly trounced in November 2020, he will be limited in his maneuvers, master in democratic negation though he may be. But in case of a slender victory by his Democratic challenger or an uncertain result, chaos beckons. Trump will not go quietly. He might not go at all.

Asked to assess the magnitude of the risk that Trump represents to orderly succession, most of the experts I consulted soberly gave it a nine on the proverbial one-to-ten scale. A former senior advisor to President Obama reflected for a moment, then gave a different answer: "Do we have an eleven?"

Note to reader: As this book heads off to press, Joe Biden has emerged as the clear front-runner in a two-man race with Bernie Sanders for the Democratic nomination. In the pages that follow, I assume that Biden emerges as the Democrats' candidate. Please excuse me if history moves faster than book production.

It's not the voting that's democracy; it's the counting.
—Tom Stoppard, *Jumpers*

PART ONE

CHAPTER 1

November 3, 2020:
The GREATEST FRAUD
in HISTORY!!

Imagine the following scenario: It's November 3, 2020, election day. The most expensive—and nastiest—presidential race in U.S. history is over. Turnout is light but only because the COVID-19 outbreak has led tens of millions to vote by absentee ballot. By the time polls close on the West Coast, the race remains too close to call. President Trump carries the crucial swing state of Ohio, keeping his chances of a second term alive. But shortly after midnight, CNN projects that Joe Biden has won Pennsylvania, giving him 283 electoral votes, 13 more than the 270 needed for victory. Wolf Blitzer announces that Biden has been elected the forty-sixth president of the United States.

The other major networks also declare Biden the winner, with one exception—Fox. At 2:00 a.m., Biden delivers a short speech to his jubilant supporters. He notes, to a chorus of boos, that President Trump has not yet called to congratulate him and expresses the hope that he will be hearing from the president shortly.

His wait is in vain; the call never comes.

In a feisty address to his supporters in the Presidential Ballroom of the Trump International Hotel in D.C., the president makes clear that he is not about to concede. "We knew they'd stop at nothing, didn't we?" Trump says. "The radicals and socialists who control the Democratic Party can't beat me fairly, and they *know* it. So now they're trying to steal *our* victory. These are bad, bad people, disgusting people. Scum—I hate to say it, but it's true, it's so true. But something tells me they're not going to get away with it, are they?"

"*No!*" the crowd calls back raucously.

"I think I see some folks here willing to fight the scum. Am I right?" Trump asks.

"*Yes!*" roars the crowd before breaking out into a chant of "*Fight! Fight! Fight!*"

The next morning, the nation awakes to a presidential Twitterstorm.

Donald J. Trump

@realDonaldTrump

Biggest SCANDAL in AMERICAN history! Rotten Dems tried to steal presidency with FAILED Mueller WITCH HUNT. They tried to steal presidency with FAILED impeachment WITCH HUNT. Now SLEEPY JOE and the CORRUPT Dems are trying to STEAL this election from the American people. I will...

* * *

Donald J. Trump

@realDonaldTrump

...fight the RIGGED result and will punish TREASONOUS CNN and failing NY Times and the Pelosi GANG responsible for worst election HOAX ever!! The TREASONOUS HATERS won't get away with the GREATEST FRAUD in HISTORY!!

And so begins a constitutional crisis of unprecedented gravity.

Of course, it may never come to this. To begin with, there is no guarantee that the American people will vote Trump out of office. He continues to enjoy fervent support among his base; he holds the same geographic Electoral College advantage he had in 2016; and he has amassed an enormous war chest of contributions to finance a campaign far more sophisticated and organized than his prior bid. While the COVID-19 pandemic has rattled financial markets and exposed the administration's failure to mount a timely response, the fact that a president who presided over three years of economic growth would even face a serious electoral challenge is a testament to how divisive and unhinged Trump's leadership has been.

But while his defeat is far from certain, what is not uncertain is how Donald Trump would react to electoral defeat, especially a narrow one. He will reject the result. Our nation needs to prepare for this scenario. Trump's refusal to accept defeat is not possible or even probable—it is all but inevitable.

CHAPTER 2

Trump Rejects Defeat

How can we make this prediction with such confidence? In February 2019, Michael Cohen ended his testimony before the House Oversight Committee with this note of alarm: "Given my experience working for Mr. Trump, I fear that if he loses the election in 2020 that there will never be a peaceful transition of power."[1] Two months later, in an interview with the *New York Times*, House Speaker Nancy Pelosi echoed this concern, warning that should Trump lose, "he's not going to respect the election."[2]

We needn't turn to Trump's former "fixer" or to the House Speaker for insight into Trump's intentions. Trump himself has essentially told the nation he will never accept defeat. In the run-up to the 2016 election, he insisted in a tweet that "there is large-scale voter fraud happening" and predicted that the election "could be 'stolen'" from him. His campaign website entreated supporters to "help me stop Crooked Hillary from rigging this election!"[3] In an August 2016 interview with Sean Hannity, Trump predicted that "the election is going to be rigged," adding, "I hope the Republicans are watching closely, or it's going to be taken away from us."[4]

Two months later, in his third and final debate with Hillary Clinton, candidate Trump refused to answer when moderator Chris

Wallace asked him whether he would "absolutely accept the result" of an electoral loss. "I'll look at it at the time," Trump responded. Reminded by Wallace that the peaceful transition of power is a critical feature of our constitutional order and essential to American political stability, Trump still refused to commit to accepting the results. "I will tell you at the time," he repeated. "I'll keep you in suspense."

The comment left Hillary Clinton visibly stunned. Calling Trump's response "horrifying," she went on to elaborate: "That is not the way our democracy works. We've been around for 240 years.... We've accepted the outcomes when we may not have liked them, and that is what must be expected of anyone standing on a debate stage during a general election."[5]

Clinton was hardly alone in her astonishment and dismay. In its post-debate coverage, MSNBC ran a chyron: "Trump Refuses to Say If He Will Accept Election Results." CNN led with virtually the same message—"Trump Won't Commit to Accepting Election Results"—while the Associated Press declared that "Trump Refuses to Say He Will Accept Election Result," and accused him of "threatening to upend a basic pillar of American democracy."[6]

The prominent American historian Douglas Brinkley went further still, describing Trump's words as "secessionist" and "revolutionary"; they were the views of a presidential candidate, Brinkley commented, "trying to topple the apple cart entirely."[7]

Most pundits, on both the left and the right, agreed that in challenging the peaceful transition of power, Trump had sealed his fate. Nicolle Wallace, an NBC News analyst and advisor to Senator John McCain's 2008 presidential campaign, said, "He may as well have laid down in his own coffin with a hammer and nail and pounded it in himself."[8]

Nonetheless, the Obama White House was sufficiently concerned by the possibility that Trump would refuse to accept defeat that senior staff convened in late October 2016 to fashion a response to the political crisis such a refusal would ignite. The plan called for congressional Republicans, former presidents, and former cabinet-level officials, including Colin Powell and Condoleezza Rice, to publicly validate Clinton's victory. They would also emphasize the conclusions of the U.S. intelligence community—namely, that the Russians had interfered with the election and had done so to favor Trump, not Clinton. The idea, as Ben Rhodes explained, was to avert any potential crisis in as bipartisan a manner as possible.[9]

CHAPTER 3

Trump Rejects Victory

While Trump's election may have spared the nation the trauma of a presidential candidate refusing to accept defeat, it presented us a no less unusual display—a president-elect challenging his victory. In January 2017, the freshly inaugurated president tweeted, "In addition to winning the Electoral College in a landslide, I won the popular vote if you deduct the millions of people who voted illegally." In the following days, Trump repeated and refined this claim, insisting that three to five million illegals threw the popular-vote count to Clinton. By way of proof, the president waved at an outlandish story: that golfing great Bernhard Langer had allegedly been barred from a polling station while others "who did not look as if they should be allowed to vote" were allowed in.[1] Never mind that American voters have no particular "look"—or that Langer, a German citizen, could not himself have legally cast a ballot in 2016; the significant story here was the specter of a freshly inaugurated president challenging the results of an election that he had *won*.

In the 2018 midterms, Trump again played the fraud card. In Florida, Republican Ron DeSantis enjoyed a slim lead in the gubernatorial race, as did Republican Rick Scott in the Senate race, but state-mandated recounts promised to erode and possibly reverse these leads. Taking to Twitter, Trump attacked the recounts, alleging, again without an iota of proof, that Democrats were committing fraud:

> The Florida Election should be called in favor of Rick Scott and Ron DeSantis in that large numbers of new ballots showed up out of nowhere, and many ballots are missing or forged. An honest vote count is no longer possible—ballots massively infected. Must go with Election Night![2]

The recounts did not overturn DeSantis's and Scott's victories, but rather confirmed them; still, the episode again revealed a Trump fully prepared to attack the integrity of the electoral process in order to get the result he wants.

CHAPTER 4

Elections the Authoritarian Way

The prospect of Trump refusing to accept electoral defeat in 2020 raises an obvious question: What would he hope to gain by challenging the system of peaceful succession?

To answer this, let me begin with an obverse question: Why would any incumbent leader ever *accept* electoral defeat? If the question sounds frivolous—if our clear answer is "Because he lost"—it's only because the astonishing stability of our constitutional order makes us see the peaceful succession of power as a natural and inevitable feature of political systems. In truth, it is anything but.

Those who have studied nations transitioning from authoritarianism to democracy have shown that it is always easier to stage the first democratic election than the second.[1] The first election is a moment of promise; it typically features a contest between persons offering bright visions of a nation's future, with no candidate enjoying a claim to leadership prior to the verdict of the people. And whatever their differences, all the candidates typically express support for the nation's fledgling democracy and pledge to eliminate the vestiges of authoritarianism.

Yet once installed in office, the new leader's enthusiasm for democratic elections begins to wane. As the next election looms, the leader is now something more than a candidate—he is an incumbent. For the incumbent, the original justification for staging an election no longer applies. The electoral process has already served its purpose—it has installed him in power. With that power comes wealth, prestige, and immense influence, not only for the incumbent himself, but for a large coterie of supporters who share in the administration of power or otherwise benefit from the largesse of the regime. For the incumbent and his supporters, the very process that brought them to power now represents a threat.

The second election looks particularly unwelcome if the incumbent has spent his term in office taking bribes, stealing from the public coffers, and misappropriating funds. In such cases, relinquishing power may be tantamount to surrendering to the criminal justice system. Deprived of his office, the former head of state may face the prospect of going from the pinnacle of power to the ignominy of prison.

The leader in office thus has powerful incentives to either postpone the election or cancel it altogether. The means at his disposal are many: He can manufacture a domestic or foreign crisis, declare a state of emergency, and suspend the normal operations of government. The nation, he solemnly announces, can ill afford an election at such a moment of crisis.

And there are subtler ways to hold on to power. Instead of canceling elections outright, prominent contemporary authoritarians such as Vladimir Putin, Recep Tayyip Erdoğan, and Viktor Orbán have, in the words of one observer, usefully deployed them "to control their populations, to divide opposition and to maintain power."[2] Here the key is not to suspend or dispense with elections but rather to "fix outcomes... through laws and policies that embed unfairness at every level" of the electoral process.[3]

Fixing elections can take a wide and imaginative range of forms.

The effort need not wait for election day; indeed, as Tip O'Neill quipped about voting, efforts to rig an election should come early and often. With control over the military, police, and intelligence and revenue services, the incumbent can order the disruption of the opposition's political rallies; he can make sure that opposition supporters are harassed and bloodied, that the opposition campaign is charged with fiscal improprieties, and that opposition candidates are blackmailed and/or publicly smeared. More ambitiously, he can arrange for opposition candidates to be arrested, detained, or even assassinated.

Come election day, the resourceful authoritarian can make sure that ballots are stuffed in his favor, that opposition strongholds lack polling places and working voting machines, and that bands of roving thugs threaten, intimidate, and beat opposition voters. Finally, he can make sure his partisans are responsible for collecting ballots and tallying the results.

Such measures remind us that, relatively speaking, Trump remains a weak authoritarian. True, his impulses and sympathies are clearly authoritarian, and he is also arguably the most powerful person on the planet. But the continued vitality of our nation's legal, constitutional, and institutional constraints have *so far* largely checked Trump's most transgressive impulses. The United States, after all, is not a transitional society lacking a vital democratic culture. Our Constitution does not have an emergency provision, like the disastrous Article 48 of the Weimar Constitution, that enabled Germany's slide into dictatorial rule.[4] Trump cannot simply bend the Constitution to his will.

Trump's weakness is also a product of his own peculiar demagogic style. Most authoritarians gather and consolidate power by building strong alliances with a nation's coercive apparatus—the military, the intelligence services, and the justice community. Trump has done none of this. Early in his presidency, he surrounded himself with generals, installing John Kelly as his chief of staff, H. R. McMaster as his national security advisor, and James Mattis as his secretary of defense, but none proved capable of working productively with the president. In resigning his post, Mattis publicly rebuked Trump for his failure to treat allies with respect and to deal with malign actors aggressively.[5] Far from supporting him, most top brass in the military either distrust the president or oppose him, directly or indirectly.

Things are even more toxic in the case of the intelligence services and the Department of Justice. Trump has loudly disparaged the FBI, the CIA, and the Justice Department. To widespread astonishment, he rejected the conclusions of his own intelligence agencies regarding Russian interference in the 2016 election, and instead chose to trust assurances coming from an adversary's president. And not just any adversary. When Trump asked Ukrainian president Volodymyr Zelensky to look into the possibility that it was Ukraine and not Russia that had hacked into the Democratic National Committee's emails in 2016, he was indulging a conspiracy theory manufactured and peddled by the Russian intelligence service itself.[6] While rejecting—even ridiculing—the conclusions of his own intelligence agencies, Trump has embraced a conspiracy theory hatched by the very intelligence service that criminally tampered with our election system.

Such attitudes and actions find no precedent in American presidential history. Also without precedent is the ill repute in which Trump, not coincidentally, is held by members of the CIA, the FBI, and the Department of Justice. In William Barr, Trump has found an attorney general willing to act as the president's private advocate, something that even Jeff Sessions refused to do. Still, the fact remains that a great number of Justice Department lawyers find the president contemptible; and beyond merely despising Trump, many officials in these bureaucracies do not believe that he is dedicated to protecting America's interests. Let us not forget that his impeachment was triggered by a CIA whistleblower.

A strong authoritarian—a Putin, say—would command his own intelligence services to dig up dirt on his political opponents. Trump, by contrast, had to lean on a foreign power to do his dirty work; not only could he not depend on intelligence officials to aid and abet his corruption, but in fact he found himself called out by persons nominally under his direct command. This is a remarkable state of affairs, and one that underscores how broadly and intensely Trump is reviled by the very agencies that a strong authoritarian can most dependably rely on for support.

Such limitations notwithstanding, Trump has done his best to play the strongman. Before the 2018 midterms, borrowing a page from the Putin-Erdoğan-Orbán playbook, he declared a sham emergency, claiming that America was facing an invasion of Latinx migrants that warranted the dispatch of five thousand troops to the southern border. (After the election, warnings of the impending invasion dwindled, and the troops were quietly withdrawn.) Trump has also gleefully adopted the standard authoritarian practice of branding opponents as enemies and criminals. Three years into his presidency, he continues to reprise his vicious 2016 treatment of Hillary Clinton, routinely inciting supporters to chants of "Lock her up!" His response to his impeachment marked a significant escalation in his rhetorical attacks. He likened the CIA whistleblower to a "spy" who, in the "old days," would have been executed.[7] He charged Adam Schiff, the Democratic chair of the House Intelligence Committee, with treason, a capital offense.

Trump is clearly prepared to deploy authoritarian tactics to suppress the vote of minorities. On the day before the 2018 midterms, he tweeted that "Law Enforcement has been strongly notified to watch closely for any ILLEGAL VOTING," warning further, "Anyone caught will be subject to the Maximum Criminal Penalties allowed by law."[8] The idea that police and ICE agents will be widely dispatched looking for "suspicious" voters can serve only to discourage persons of color from voting. Naturalized citizens, particularly those of Latinx heritage, might also choose not to vote, fearful of being harassed by law enforcement or by aggressive Trump supporters.

Finally, we know that Trump has already solicited interference in the 2020 race. Recall that Trump made the notorious phone call to Ukrainian president Zelensky exactly one day after loudly proclaiming that Robert Mueller's doddering appearance on Capitol Hill provided evidence of his complete exoneration from the charge of collusion. Trump's narrow escape from accountability only fueled his brazenness. Having survived impeachment, Trump has no reason to second-guess the wisdom of inviting further foreign interference—provided, of course, that such interference works to his benefit.

It is probable, then, that Trump will call upon a range of authoritarian techniques to try to manufacture an electoral victory in 2020. This should be a source of alarm to all Americans, but it is not the primary focus of our attention, which remains less the possibility that Trump will steal victory than that he will reject defeat. That this is our chief concern reminds us once more of Trump's weak authoritarianism. A more powerful authoritarian would never let himself get into this situation in the first place; he would have already so corrupted the process that his chance of losing would have been effectively eliminated.

Should Trump, however, succeed in an act of electoral nullification, he would propel himself into the ranks of Putin, Erdoğan, and Orbán—the leaders he appears to most admire. More to the point, he would inflict a grave, historic, and perhaps fatal wound to our constitutional democracy. That this is no longer a far-fetched fantasy shows us just how deformed our political landscape has become.

CHAPTER 5

The Peculiar Beauty of Conceding Defeat

The ominous prospect of a president prepared to nullify an election raises a basic question. Given the advantages of remaining in office, why have American incumbents historically accepted electoral defeat? The answer is both simple and profound: Our political leaders have accepted—and internalized—the norms of the democratic process.

To appreciate what this means, we need to note the difference between *conceding* and *submitting to* defeat. Conceding defeat is a *normative* act. In recognizing the legitimacy of his defeat, the conceding candidate acknowledges—and accepts—that his opponent has fairly earned victory. Submitting to defeat, by contrast, is merely a tactical, de facto recognition that further fight is futile.

The contested presidential election of 2000 provides an important and even stirring example of the power of our norms. As we recall, the race between George W. Bush and Al Gore turned on the outcome in Florida, where balloting errors amid an improbably close contest made for chaos. Thirty-five days after the nation had gone to the polls, the count—and with it the national election—remained

unresolved. Then, with Bush clinging to a 537-vote lead out of six
million cast statewide, the Supreme Court suddenly stopped the
Florida recount, effectively handing Bush victory.

It was a dramatic action, and a controversial one. Yet we would
be wrong to credit the Supreme Court with bringing needed closure
to the 2000 election. That credit goes to Vice President Al Gore.
On December 13, the day after the Court issued its ruling, Gore
conceded, striking this graceful note:

> History gives us many examples of contests as hotly debated, as
> fiercely fought, with their own challenges to the popular will.
> Other disputes dragged on for weeks before reaching resolution,
> and each time both victor and vanquished have accepted the
> result peacefully and in a spirit of reconciliation. So be it with us.[1]

Nothing compelled Gore to concede. He could have asked the
Florida Supreme Court to ignore the Supreme Court's ruling. As we
shall see, he could have taken his case to Congress, the body constitutionally charged with tabulating and accepting the votes of the
Electoral College. Indeed, had Gore carried the fight to Congress, he,
as president of the Senate, would have presided over the debate. Not
only did Gore refrain from doing so, but he specifically instructed
Democrats in Congress not to challenge the Florida results.

Why? No law compelled him to accept the Court's result; nothing in the Constitution demanded his concession. In fact, members
of his own legal team encouraged him to push the fight, and many
Democratic senators, such as Barbara Boxer, deeply regretted not
challenging the Florida vote.[2] Nonetheless, Gore chose to accept the
legitimacy of a Court decision that was widely attacked as dreadfully
reasoned and transparently partisan. In doing so, he placed the good
of the country over his own personal interest in winning.

In saying this, I do not mean to cast Al Gore as a person of extraordinary decency or selflessness. He might well have these qualities, but that is not what he evinced in accepting the Court's decision. A constitutional democracy does not require or even expect its leaders to be extraordinarily good people; James Madison acknowledged as much in his canonical *Federalist* No. 10. What the system does expect is that our leaders have internalized the norms that make the democratic process work. And that is what Gore demonstrated by conceding.

Gore's action reminds us of an essential truth: *Our Constitution does not secure the peaceful transition of power, but rather presupposes it.* The peaceful transition is a background condition of democratic governance, a condition created and maintained through tradition and norms. A democracy cannot exist without leaders who respect these norms. In conceding, Gore did nothing heroic. He simply demonstrated the force of the norms that make constitutional democracy possible. In fact, it is probably wrong to think of Gore choosing to concede, in the sense of weighing competing alternatives in a cost/benefit calculation. That is not how norms influence the decision-making process. Norms place moral ballast on decision-making; they take certain options off the table. Gore had internalized the norms of constitutional democracy, and so it was largely unthinkable that he would do otherwise than concede.

That said, it is also true that our political leaders have accepted electoral defeat because they have nothing to gain by refusing to do so; there is little point to mounting a costly challenge to an electoral result if the prospects of success are remote. To be sure, it is precisely the normative understandings cited above that have made such challenges seem fruitless. Political actors will not risk provoking a crisis of transition if they believe they will only succeed in turning themselves into national pariahs.

CHAPTER 6

So Much for Our Norms

Now we turn to President Trump. What restraining force do norms play in his political calculations? The short, dispiriting, and irrefutable answer is—none. Where other politicians have demonstrated a willingness to push against these norms, Trump has simply ignored them altogether, smashing through the guardrails meant to channel political discourse toward democratic civility.

Even more shocking than Trump's disregard of the norms of constitutional democracy are the rewards he has garnered for doing so. As we've noted, norms define the limits of appropriate behavior; when someone violates them, we expect the violator to pay a price. Not so in Trump's case. For instance, one norm of our political culture is that political leaders hold war heroes in high regard. When Trump disparaged John McCain for having been a POW in Vietnam, pundits predicted that he would suffer for his reckless comments, just as they predicted that his refusal to say he would accept a Clinton victory in 2016 would prove politically fatal. But not only did he not pay a price, he was politically rewarded—indeed, we can say he reaped the greatest political reward imaginable. He was elected president.

Trump's success has revealed something exceptionally worrisome about the norms that underpin our democratic order. At the very least, we must ask why, far from paying a political price, Trump has been largely if not consistently rewarded for trampling on them. Consider his impeachment, which should have exacted a high political cost. After all, Trump is only the third president in our nation's history to face this extraordinary form of censure.[1] In the short term, at least, it appears that the president actually benefited from the attempt to remove him, as some came to see it as a needless exercise in partisanship, while others appeared to view it as an attempt to make an end-run around the electoral process. True, tens of millions of Americans continue to consider Trump a disgrace, unfit for office. Yet he survived his impeachment thanks to the steadfast support of Republican lawmakers who are prepared to defend and condone his disregard for the rules of constitutional government and congressional oversight.

Let us note the obvious—that Trump's success would be unthinkable in the media environment of even a generation ago, when major newspapers and three television networks curated the news into an acceptable normative framework. Today, the likes of Breitbart, *Fox & Friends*, Sean Hannity, and Rush Limbaugh can thrive by catering to and cultivating extreme partisanship. Far from placing a check on Trump's transgressions, these outlets provide him with the kind of truculent, reflexive support associated with state-run TV in Putin's Russia. This dynamic brings us back to the matter of prudence. We have observed that a candidate will presumably submit to defeat if launching an aggressive challenge will risk making himself a pariah. But here again Trump is not your normal—or norm-abiding—politician. *Success has a different meaning and valence for him.*

Let's return to the election of 2016. What on earth could Trump have possibly hoped to gain by refusing to accept the result, had he lost? In 2020, a refusal to accept defeat might reflect the fact that

Trump could face indictment for obstruction of justice the moment he vacates office. The federal crime of obstruction is governed by a five-year statute of limitations, and in 2020, prosecutors will be well within this statutory period, but by 2024, the deadline for bringing charges will have passed.[2] Trump arguably now has sound reasons for wanting to remain in office.

None of this applied in the 2016 election. Indeed, a steady stream of Trump insiders who have gone on to write scathing accounts of their erstwhile boss report that Trump wasn't even particularly interested in getting elected and in fact anticipated defeat. And yet Trump showed himself willing to radically reject such a defeat, potentially at great cost to the nation. Why? Robert Reich, Bill Clinton's former secretary of labor, has characterized Trump as "pathologically incapable of admitting defeat,"[3] a sentiment echoed by many commentators outlining this or that aspect of his alleged psychopathology. And yet we need not avail ourselves of the *DSM-V* to explain Trump's behavior; indeed, in what sense can we call behavior that is so richly rewarded pathological? To repeat behavior that garners rewards can hardly be described as irrational; to the contrary, it is the very definition of rational behavior. And what are these rewards? Money, power, attention, and the seamless connections among them.

In this triumvirate of worldly rewards, Trump's relationship to power is perhaps the most interesting. Donald Trump does not care about political power conventionally conceived. Many political leaders have craved power while keeping a low profile; Dick Cheney comes to mind. Others have cultivated the adoration of crowds, but principally as a means of consolidating political power—think Hitler. Trump, by contrast, seeks power simply to keep himself in the public eye; or to put it differently, the only power Trump really craves is the power to command attention.

Consider, for instance, the "social media summit" Trump convened in July 2019 that brought leading right-wing bloggers, blowhards, and conspiracy theorists to the White House. During this "summit," Trump reflected on some of his own most inflammatory tweets—such as his claim that then-president Obama had bugged his phone. He did not retract his baseless and defamatory claim, nor did he defend it. Rather, he expressed something like wonder at his ability to create news out of nothing.[4] By his own admission, he is mesmerized by his power to dominate the news cycle by manufacturing controversy.

To a degree and in a manner unprecedented in American presidential history, Trump thrives on mayhem. He presides over a White House characterized by a truly remarkable level of chaos and dysfunction. In this regard, Trump does in fact bear a passing resemblance to Hitler. A myth of the Third Reich was that it was tightly organized and efficiently run. This is far from the truth; Hitler was a chaotic leader, who thrived on playing his ministers and advisors off one another. The similarities extend further. Hitler was a political parvenu who viewed his own improbable political ascendency as evidence of his infallible genius. He often changed his mind, either through uncertainty or to keep both enemies and intimates guessing about his intentions. And he routinely solicited advice only to ignore it completely, convinced that he alone knew better. Such behavior is familiar to Americans who have chafed—or thrived—under Trump's erratic leadership.

Trump's connection to chaos and mayhem goes well beyond management style. He draws energy and sustenance from chaos. His power to spread chaos keeps him at the center of attention—and remaining there is his principal political aim. This returns us to 2016. Had he lost, Trump surely would have made good on his threat not to concede. But this does not mean that he would have unleashed a gaggle of lawyers, tasked with bringing suits challenging election results in various states. Overturning Clinton's victory and gaining office would not have been his aim. For Trump, the goal was not to be president but to burnish the brand. And his brand did not need victory; all it required was that Trump's voters believe their man had been cheated out of victory.

In this way, Trump was guaranteed to emerge a winner, even if he lost the election. In defeat, he would have preserved—or even enhanced—his heroic stature among his supporters. Anticipating defeat, he evidently weighed launching his own television network with Sean Hannity.[5] In his new role as network director and political avatar, he could have continued to attack the system and President Clinton; he could have spread innuendo and conspiracy theories and made himself relevant by doing what he does best—making mayhem and taking responsibility for nothing. In defeat, he would have remained the center of American political attention.

That is what Trump hoped to gain in 2016. What about 2020? We've already noted that incumbency alters the calculus in fundamental ways, and that Trump arguably has compelling prudential reasons to stay in office. But more compelling still is the fact that for a sitting president, an electoral defeat represents an especially stinging personal rebuke. In 2016, Trump was expected to lose. Not so in 2020. This time, the protection of the brand demands victory. Defeat is not an option.

This reality should trouble anyone who cares about American democracy, especially when we consider that whatever damage candidate Trump could have done to our democracy by losing in 2016 would pale in comparison to what a sitting president can wreak by rejecting defeat. A president who succeeds in remaining in power in the face of an electoral loss has staged a *coup*. Coups happen with depressing regularity in much of the world. But not here. Since George Washington left office more than 220 years ago, the peaceful transition of power has been a signature of American democracy. We have never had a suspended or delayed presidential election, not during foreign wars, not even during the Civil War. Trump threatens to upend this tradition.

CHAPTER 7

Lies, Damn Lies, and Meta-lies

We have observed that democratic norms have no purchase on Donald Trump—indeed, he gained the presidency by flouting them—and that his actions follow a coherent and simple logic: He will do whatever is necessary to protect and extend his brand. Trump doesn't need to win in 2020 in order to remain in power, but rather the opposite: He needs to remain in power to prove that he is a winner. So how might he go about engineering electoral defiance?

Our answer does not require a great deal of speculation. As we have seen, Trump already telegraphed his strategy in 2016. By falsely and recklessly attacking the integrity of our electoral system, he has already laid the groundwork for launching a challenge to the peaceful transition of power.

Trump is hardly the first liar to inhabit the White House. In an essay called "Truth and Politics," the great political thinker Hannah Arendt observed that what distinguishes democratic from authoritarian regimes is not necessarily the greater honesty of democratic politicians. Politicians in all systems lie; indeed, Arendt dryly observed that "lies have always been regarded as necessary and justifiable tools...of the statesman's trade."[1]

But Trump has elevated lying from a mere tool of governance into its first principle. Members of his own staff have described him as a habitual and shameless liar. The *Washington Post* has kept a running tally of false statements made by Trump since taking office, and the number was over sixteen thousand as of this writing (March 2020).[2] Yet here again we must resist calling him a pathological liar. To do so, as some, such as the *New York Times* columnist Charles Blow, have done,[3] is to show a lack of compassion for those who suffer from this obscure malady. Pathological liars lie even when the truth would better serve them; they lie out of compulsion, not out of self-interest. Trump may be a reflexive liar, but he is not a pathological liar; lying is simply his default method of defending or advancing his interest.

One could write a book inventorying Trump's rich profusion of lies. In a Rose Garden ceremony in July 2019 held for signing a bill funding permanent care for 9/11 first responders, Trump announced that he had "spent a lot of time down there with you"—that is, with firefighters, police officers, and other first responders who arrived at Ground Zero.[4]

In a less warped political landscape, such a falsehood would register as astonishing and scandalous. Here is a president falsely claiming to have stood side by side with those who risked their lives and health in the days and months after the worst terrorist attack in American history. I will call such Trumpian falsehoods "first-order" lies. These are his lies about people or events. They claim a something when there was a nothing, or a nothing when there was a something. Take another example. During a campaign rally in North Carolina in the summer of 2019, Trump was in the middle of denouncing the Democratic congresswoman Ilhan Omar of Minnesota when the crowd broke out into a spontaneous chant of "Send her back!" Speaking the next day in the Oval Office, Trump insisted that he had been displeased with the chant and had tried to stop it. "I started speaking very quickly," he claimed. This was demonstrably false.[5] A video of the event made clear that Trump did nothing to stop the crowd, but instead stood in silence for some ten seconds, looking rather pleased while the chant reverberated around him.

Compare this first-order lie to Trump's tweet from September 2, 2019:

> The LameStream Media has gone totally CRAZY! They write whatever they want, seldom have sources (even though they say they do), never do "fact checking" anymore, and are only looking for the "kill." They take good news and make it bad. They are now beyond Fake, they are Corrupt.[6]

This tweet also contains multiple lies, but of a different variety. Call them "second-order" lies, or "meta-lies." Such lies attack the very institutions vouchsafed with examining the truthfulness of politicians' statements. Democracies require the existence of neutral, politically independent institutions capable of safeguarding truth from the politics of prevarication. These institutions subject the statements and actions of members of government to critical analysis. In this way, citizens can make informed choices at the polls. In so doing, these institutions enable democratic self-governance.

Trump's meta-lies defame the very institutions that provide such an independent check on the government—and on the president. He has attacked federal judges, most notoriously when he claimed, in 2016, that U.S. district court judge Gonzalo Curiel had an "inherent conflict of interest"—namely, a Mexican family background—in presiding over a lawsuit against the now defunct Trump University. In November 2018, Trump attacked a federal judge who had ruled against an administration attempt to bar anyone crossing the U.S.-Mexico border from receiving asylum; the ruling, according to Trump, was "a disgrace" committed by "an Obama judge."[7]

While federal court decisions do at times track the ideology of the president who appointed the judge, that fact by no means shows judicial neutrality to be a myth or that judges behave simply as pure partisans. To say so—as Trump does whenever a ruling displeases him—is to radically deny the existence of any institution or body within our constitutional system capable of independent judgment.

Of course, the target of Trump's most persistent meta-lies has been the free press. Imagine that back in 2015 you had been asked to identify the country whose head of state had called the free press "the enemy of the people," had lambasted journalists as "disgusting people," "crooked," "fraudulent," "corrupt," "degenerate...haters," who "constantly lie and cheat," and traffic in "garbage" and "Fake News"—and joked about doing violence to them. You might have named Turkey or Hungary or Poland or Venezuela or Russia. But the United States? Unthinkable. Now the unthinkable has become routine.

Trump's meta-lies have the character of libels—they do not simply spread falsehoods; they falsely and maliciously malign their institutional targets. He routinely claims that CNN, the *Washington Post*, and the *New York Times*, to take his favorite targets, willfully fabricate news in order to advance a partisan agenda. It is for this reason that ordinary fact-checking provides a wholly inadequate response to Trump's lying. Such fact-checking presupposes confidence in the fact-checker, trust that Trump systematically undermines. For why would I accept your fact-checking if I do not trust your testing procedures? Needed, then, would be a meta-fact-checker, an institution that examines whether the fact-checking institutions can be trusted!

Trump's meta-lies—his pervasive and dishonest claims that the very institutions empowered in a democracy to expose lies are themselves corrupt, dishonest, and lying—poison the well of democratic discourse. But the full threat they pose to the peaceful transition of power becomes clear only when viewed through the filter of his defamation of our electoral process.

CHAPTER 8

The Sweet Air of Legitimacy

The great constitutional scholar Charles Black told the story of a French priest who traveled to the United States by steamer. As his ship approached the New York skyline, the priest was said to exclaim, "It is wonderful to breathe the sweet air of legitimacy."[1]

Legitimacy, as Black understood, is the very condition of life of a democratic government. It is, as he put it, "the stability of a good government over time." In the words of another leading constitutionalist, Alexander Bickel, legitimacy expresses itself in the people's "consent to specific actions or to the authority to act...whether or not approved in each instance."[2] This is a crucial point. A government need not always do the smart, proper, or even the right thing to be considered legitimate. We may vehemently disagree with any number of policies of our government and yet still consider them to be legitimate—provided the processes that generate these policies are themselves deemed legitimate.

Elections represent the bedrock of the democratic process; they are the fundamental tool by which citizens choose those leaders vouchsafed with protecting and advancing their interests. To be sure, elections confer power, and so invite abuse; and this country certainly has not been immune to electoral fraud. In 1948, when

Lyndon Johnson was elected to the Senate from Texas, catapulting the future president into national political prominence, the victory was greased by an audacious campaign of ballot-stuffing, an act that his biographer Robert Caro memorably described as "brazen thievery."[3]

More recently, the 2018 midterms provided an egregious instance of electoral fraud. In North Carolina's 9th Congressional District, Republican Mark Harris narrowly defeated his Democratic opponent, Dan McCready, barely squeaking by in a district that partisan gerrymandering had already carved up to virtually guarantee a Republican victory. Unwilling to risk defeat even on a playing field tilted steeply in his favor, Harris's campaign went one step further, illegally procuring absentee ballots to secure a win.[4]

But if the North Carolina race provides an example of the persistence of fraud, it also demonstrates the power of corrective mechanisms. Three months after the midterms, North Carolina's board of elections, citing "corruption" and clear evidence of "a tainted election," tossed out the results and ordered a new contest.[5] The effort to steal the election failed.

North Carolina's tainted election also remains something of an outlier. In recent decades, federal elections have been relatively free of the more blatant forms of fraud. More persistently, our elections continue to be vexed by campaigns to disenfranchise racial and ethnic minorities and the urban poor. Adopting strict voter ID laws that claim to safeguard the integrity of the process, Republican lawmakers in numerous states have systematically worked to strip the vote from groups that overwhelmingly support Democrats.

Trump's attacks on the integrity of our electoral process have an altogether different cast. He maligns processes that are actually functioning properly and so panders to those who *perceive them as corrupt*. Until recently, such misperceptions have remained the province of conspiracy theorists and fringe extremist groups. No longer. Trump has mainstreamed these views. For the first time in our history we have the president of the United States routinely insisting that the democratic process cannot be trusted. That such destabilizing attacks would emanate from the White House presents a new and toxic threat to democratic legitimacy.

Trump's war of perception against our electoral system bears many of the same hallmarks of his war against the Mueller investigation. Through a storm of tweets attacking that investigation as a partisan inquisition, Trump primed his supporters to reject its results before they were even published. In these efforts, he proved successful: A March 2019 poll found that half the respondents agreed with the president that the Mueller probe was a "witch hunt."[6]

Since 2016, Trump has likewise prepared his supporters to reject any electoral outcome in which he loses. And yet we can only fully appreciate the scope and power of the president's attacks on electoral integrity when we combine them with his meta-lies about the news media. Trump insists we cannot trust the results of the electoral process, and further, that we cannot trust the media sources tasked with telling us whether those results can be trusted. What he has done is to strip us—or, rather, his supporters—of any independent basis for assessing the truth or falseness of a claim of fraud. His lies have eroded confidence in our elections, and his meta-lies have done the same for our principal media outlets. If neither the process nor the device for assessing the trustworthiness of the process can be trusted, then we are left with nothing—except the word of the leader.

As with the attacks on the special counsel's investigation, Trump's perceptual war on the media and the electoral process has proven disturbingly effective. A report published in June 2019 showed that nearly half of Americans doubt the fairness of independent fact-checkers. The split is particularly dramatic along party lines: 70 percent of Republicans say fact-checkers tend to favor one side, compared with only 29 percent of Democrats.[7]

In the case of the so-called mainstream media, the numbers are more dramatic still, with an astonishing 89 percent of Republicans describing the media as unfairly biased. And it's not simply a matter of distrust. Using rhetoric reminiscent of Stalin, President Trump has notoriously defamed journalists as "the enemy of the people." Most Republicans apparently agree. In 2017, a Cato Free Speech and Tolerance Survey found that nearly two-thirds of Republicans (63 percent) believe that journalists are the enemy.[8]

Alarmingly, a substantial percentage of Republicans support giving the president the power to control the mainstream media. A study released in August 2018 reported that a plurality of Republicans (43 percent) agreed with the statement that "the president should have the authority to close news outlets engaged in bad behavior." The report concluded on what it described as a "somewhat reassuring" note—that "less than a quarter of Republicans [23 percent]" agree that "President Trump should close down mainstream news outlets, like CNN, the *Washington Post* and the *New York Times*."[9] *Somewhat reassuring?* We are to feel reassured that only one in four Republicans support essentially gutting the First Amendment?

We find a parallel erosion of faith in the integrity of the electoral process among Republicans. In a survey carried out prior to the 2016 election, 84 percent of Republican voters said they believed a "meaningful amount of fraud occurred in American elections," with nearly 60 percent of GOP voters saying they believed "illegals" would "vote in meaningful amounts" in November 2016.[10] An even greater number—nearly three out of every four Republicans—believed the election could be stolen from Trump. No less disturbing are the results of a poll taken in July 2017—more than six months after the election—which showed that nearly half of Republicans (47 percent) believed Trump won the 2016 popular vote.[11]

How are we to make sense of that result? It is possible that some of those polled simply do not understand that our system of presidential elections can produce an Electoral College victor who loses the national popular vote. The more unsettling explanation is that nearly half of all Republicans believe massive fraud cost Trump the national popular vote. Shockingly, a poll from July 2017 showed that 52 percent of Republicans would support Trump's postponing the 2020 election "until the country can make sure that only eligible American voters can vote."[12] We've observed that even the Civil War did not disturb our history of regularly scheduled elections.[13] What's distressing about this result is not merely that a majority of Republicans would now support a delay; it's that they would entrust Trump with the decision.

It is hard to exaggerate the danger that such views represent, especially at a time when a health emergency could create the pretext for a delay in voting. Confidence in electoral results is the foundation of orderly succession. If people distrust the process and the trustworthiness of the results, then a leader's insidious act of electoral defiance can be spun as a heroic defense of the system. This would doubtless be Trump's tactic in 2020: constitutional usurpation packaged as an act of democratic preservation.

CHAPTER 9

Bootstrapping Meta-lies into
Institutional Realities

We began by asking how Trump might engineer a radical act of electoral nullification, and have observed that his lies and meta-lies have already laid the groundwork for such an act by defaming the integrity of the electoral process and the trustworthiness of those reporting on that process.

Disturbing as this is, Trump has gone a good deal further, demonstrating a capacity to bootstrap lies into institutional realities. On his third day in office, when he first floated the falsehood that "between three million and five million illegal votes caused me to lose the popular vote," many observers dismissed this as no more than a display of the extravagant narcissism that led the new president, in the face of undeniable visual evidence to the contrary, to insist that his inaugural crowds had been larger than Obama's.

In fact, the falsehood signaled a more ambitious political agenda. This became clear a few months later, in May 2017, when the president announced the creation of the Presidential Advisory Commission on Election Integrity. We know Russia launched a "sweeping and systematic" campaign to influence the outcome of the 2016

election through a variety of criminal acts, but instead of focusing
on the all too real and persistent threats to the system coming from
foreign adversaries, the president's commission instead pursued a
bogeyman purely of its own making: the phantom problem of voter
fraud. According to one expert, only thirty-one cases of imperson-
ation fraud—that is, an ineligible voter trying to pass himself off as
an eligible—have been documented in the United States out of over
a billion votes cast between 2000 and 2014.[1] These realities notwithstanding, the commission was designed to use the myth of widespread fraud as a pretext for advocating strict voter ID laws—laws
designed, as we've mentioned, to disenfranchise racial and ethnic
minorities and the urban poor.

Vice President Mike Pence, who served as chair of the twelve-
person commission, sought early on to assure the public that the
group had not prejudged the issue, and that it would simply seek to
discover whether the allegations of sweeping fraud were true. But the
reassurance rang hollow—launching an official probe into a non-
existent problem alone suggests that the problem is real. We saw
a similar logic at work in Trump's effort to pressure Ukraine into
announcing an investigation into the Bidens. The outcome of the
investigation was of little consequence; indeed, Trump didn't even
care whether the Bidens were investigated. What he wanted was an
announcement of an official probe.

While Pence was the nominal chair, running the show was the
vice chair of the commission, Kris Kobach, a former Kansas secretary of state and the only election official of any note to insist
that Trump was "absolutely correct" in claiming that illegal votes
accounted for his popular-vote loss to Hillary Clinton.[2] In a column in Breitbart, Kobach claimed to have "proof" that the presidential contest in New Hampshire was "likely changed through
voter fraud." Citing evidence purporting to show that thousands of

persons with out-of-state driver's licenses invaded the Granite State, Kobach asserted that these fraudulent voters swung the election in favor of Clinton. "If the presidential contest had been closer," he portentously noted, "then this voter fraud might have had extraordinary consequences."[3]

And yet Kobach's proof was bogus. In response to the allegations, New Hampshire's secretary of state dutifully explained that New Hampshire law permits domiciled out-of-staters, such as college students, to vote—those thousands of "fraudulent" votes had in fact been legally cast. Breitbart published no correction to Kobach's incendiary and false claims. Instead, using a formulation that could serve as a template for every variety of denialism—from climate change to the Holocaust—Kobach insisted, "Until further research is done, we will never know the answer regarding the legitimacy of this particular election."[4] To this day, he insists that "we will probably never know" who won the popular vote in 2016.[5]

The commission included a virtual who's who of voter-fraud mythmongers. There was Heritage Foundation fellow Hans von Spakovsky, who described as "very disturbing" the news that the commission might be "bipartisan and include Democrats."[6] Joining Spakovsky was J. Christian Adams, a lawyer formerly with the Department of Justice, who had directed efforts to purge voters from eligibility rolls.[7] And there was Ken Blackwell, the former Ohio secretary of state. In 2004, while also serving as co-chair of the Bush-Cheney campaign in Ohio, Blackwell had spearheaded a campaign, later rescinded under pressure, to reject all voter registration forms not printed on "white, uncoated paper of not less than 80 lb. text weight."[8] A subsequent report entitled *What Went Wrong in Ohio: The Conyers Report on the 2004 Presidential Election*, prepared by the Democratic staff of the House Judiciary Committee, judged him responsible for "intentional misconduct and illegal behavior."[9]

Fortunately, the Pence-Kobach commission proved short-lived. Described by a senior White House advisor as a "shit show,"[10] the commission was matched in its fraudulence only by its incompetence. Operating in secrecy, it demanded that all states send it their voter registration lists, including voters' personal information and Social Security numbers. The request was so alarmingly overbroad that it met with bipartisan opposition, prompting the Mississippi secretary of state, Republican Delbert Hosemann, to tell the commission to "jump in the Gulf of Mexico."[11] Opposition to the sweeping request resulted in numerous lawsuits; tied up in litigation, the commission failed to issue the report it was tasked to produce, and in early 2018 it was disbanded. A few months later, a federal court struck down Kansas's strict voter ID law, specifically rebuking Kobach for his "repeated and flagrant violations of disclosure and discovery rules."[12]

The collapse of the Pence-Kobach commission was certainly welcome; still, the undertaking alone was alarming, less because the commission was prepared to pursue a blatantly partisan end than because it was willing to do so by supporting Trump's defamations of the electoral process. Predictably, Trump spun the ignominious demise of his commission as further evidence that the "system is rigged"—once again alchemizing a political failure into a false indictment.

CHAPTER 10

The System Cannot Protect Itself

We have made the disturbing but confident prediction that anything short of a clear and emphatic defeat in 2020 will embolden Trump to either reject an electoral loss outright or, in the case of an uncertain result, refuse to accept any outcome other than victory. Could he succeed in such an unprecedented act of electoral nullification? How well equipped is our system to repulse such an attack?

The impressive stability that our system of presidential succession has demonstrated for over two centuries might suggest we are very well prepared. Alas, we are not. That we have largely avoided electoral disasters has more to do with our democratic culture and the character of those seeking public office than with any inherent strengths of the electoral system itself. In fact, the peculiar way by which we elect a president is tailor-made for exploitation by an authoritarian intent on causing mayhem. To understand this point moving forward, we need to keep in mind three looming dates: November 3, 2020; December 14, 2020; and January 6, 2021.

Citizens heading to the polls on November 3, 2020, will do so in the belief that they are casting their ballots for Donald Trump, Joe Biden, or some other candidate of choice. In fact, though, they will be voting not directly for this or that candidate, but for a slate of electors pledged to him, who will go on to cast their votes six weeks later. Chosen by state party officials, the electors are typically party-faithful, big-donor muckety-mucks who are otherwise completely unknown to the public.

Each state is awarded Electoral College votes equal to that state's total representation in Congress. Pennsylvania, for example, has eighteen members of the House of Representatives and, like all states, two senators, and so has twenty electoral votes. These votes operate on a winner-take-all basis; should Biden carry the popular vote in Pennsylvania, even by the narrowest of margins, he will win all twenty of the state's Electoral College votes. Come December 14, 2020, Biden's slate of twenty electors will gather in the statehouse in Harrisburg and cast their votes. (A federal law from 1948 has declared "the first Monday after the second Wednesday in December" as the date when the Electoral College casts its votes.)

This same ritual will play itself out in every state capital and in Washington, D.C. (The Twenty-Third Amendment, adopted in 1961, awarded the District, which has no congressional representation, three electoral votes.) The certified results from every state and D.C. will then be quaintly sent by registered mail to the president of the Senate—that is, Vice President Pence.[1] By the terms of the Twelfth Amendment, Congress will convene in a joint session to count the votes and declare a winner. This is set by law for January 6 following the election—in 2021, a Wednesday. To be elected, a candidate must receive at least 270 Electoral College votes, representing a bare majority of the total number of votes, 538. Should neither candidate receive a majority, as was the case in 1800 and 1824, the election would move to the House of Representatives, which would then be tasked with electing the next president. The Senate, however, would elect the vice president.

Some of this may sound unfamiliar. December 14? January 6?

The overwhelming majority of Americans remain unaware that anything of importance happens on those days. Only one day registers—election day. It is on election day that our votes are cast; CNN and MSNBC and Fox declare a winner, and that is that. This is certainly what happens in the normal run of things. But in the case of a very close result, these other dates suddenly loom large. As we cast our gaze to the 2020 contest, we will have to pay close attention to what happens on them to appreciate how an electoral crisis might take shape and dangerously escalate.

What will become clear is that once such a crisis ignites, the Constitution and federal law will prove powerless to contain it. To the contrary, defects in both constitutional and legislative design are likely to enable a defiant Trump and his supporters to push the nation toward a complete electoral meltdown.

PART TWO

CHAPTER 11

The Electoral College Revisited, Alas

The Electoral College is our constitutional appendix, a vestigial organ that has ceased to perform any valuable function and can only create problems for the body politic. It is a deservedly unloved part of our Constitution. Recently asked what part of the Constitution she would most like to alter, Justice Ruth Bader Ginsburg quickly answered, "The Electoral College—I'd like to see it abolished."[1] Most Americans agree. No poll conducted over the past seventy years has found a majority of Americans supporting it.[2] Only roughly one-third of those polled in 2019 "would prefer to keep" it.[3]

No one tasked with crafting a system of presidential election today would come up with anything remotely like the Electoral College. American jurists, who played an instrumental role in fashioning the postwar constitutions of Germany and Japan, never considered imposing one on those fledgling democracies. And not one of the new democracies created after the unraveling of the Soviet Union has sought to emulate the American electoral system.[4]

For good reason: We alone among the world's democracies have a system of presidential election that can choose the *loser* of the popular vote and place him in the highest political office in the land. While the entire twentieth century passed without such an epic misfiring, it has happened already twice in this century—first in 2000, when Al Gore received half a million more votes than George W. Bush, and again in 2016.[5]

Nor can 2000 and 2016 be dismissed as statistical aberrations. Given present-day political and demographic realities, experts estimate the current chance of the popular-vote loser winning an electoral majority as roughly one in three.[6] Indeed, those who predict Trump's reelection in 2020 expect him to once again lose the popular vote—perhaps by an even larger margin than his three-million-vote loss to Clinton in 2016.

Let us pause over the misfires in 2000 and 2016. Is it a coincidence that the two presidents who emerged from them must be reckoned as two of the worst in American history? No sooner had the affable, incurious, and inept Bush-43 been enshrined by leading presidential historians as the worst chief executive in our nation's history[7] than came his rapid rehabilitation via the advent of Trump, who has carved out a standard of malfeasance, corruption, incompetence, and dysfunction all his own.

True, the mere fact of a democratic majority provides no guaranteed bulwark against stupidity, intolerance, or hate. Alexis de Tocqueville famously warned of the dangers posed by a tyranny of the majority, and as others have observed, the rise of fascism in Europe between 1915 and 1935 revealed that "democratic processes were not only incapable of resisting the antidemocratic onslaught, but actually facilitated its ascent."[8] Recall Joseph Goebbels's gleeful observation: "This will always remain one of the best jokes of democracy, that it gave its deadly enemies the means by which it was destroyed."[9] Yet the fact remains that at no point did the Nazis ever actually win a majority of German voters. In July 1932 they captured 37 percent of the vote, but half a year later, in fresh elections, the Nazis garnered two million *fewer* votes, their overall share of the popular vote dropping to 33 percent. Once installed as chancellor, Hitler called for fresh elections in the hope of receiving an outright majority, but despite a campaign of intimidation and violence directed at opposition parties, the Nazis still fell well short of expectations, receiving 44 percent of the vote.[10] Thereafter, Hitler did away with elections altogether. So while electoral majorities may provide no safeguard against demagogues, it seems fair to say that it is harder to convince 50 percent of the electorate to embrace a politics of division and intolerance than it is to convince 40 percent.

This capacity to epically misfire is only one of the Electoral College's many problems. If the first virtue of an electoral system is the transparency of its processes, the Electoral College must be judged a failure. Most Americans have only the vaguest knowledge of how it functions. (When I ask my students at Amherst if they understand how the system can make a winner of the popular-vote loser, many confess they do not.) A system opaque to its users is one in need of change.

And yet the Electoral College is virtually impossible to get rid of. Altering or abolishing it would require a constitutional amendment, and the process of amending the Constitution is no less dysfunctional than the Electoral College itself. Scholars have concluded that ours is perhaps the most difficult to amend of all constitutions currently in operation in the world.[11] There are good reasons to make a constitution hard to change—if too easily amended, it becomes no different from a piece of ordinary legislation. But our Constitution errs too far in the other direction. And in the case of the Electoral College, which gives disproportionate power to precisely those smaller states that would have to ratify its elimination, the chance of abolition is virtually nil.

Which is why those seeking to change the system now pursue legislative end runs. Currently forty-eight states hand all their electoral votes to the winner of the state's popular vote. Maine and Nebraska are the only states with a different system—they award their electoral votes not based on the statewide contest but on results within their congressional districts.[12] In 2016, for example, Hillary Clinton received one electoral vote for carrying Maine's 1st Congressional District, while Trump received one vote for carrying the state's 2nd District. Advocates of awarding electoral votes based on the district winner rather than the state winner argue that this would make our presidential electoral system more democratic.

If only it were that simple. First, it is difficult to get states to sign on to the district scheme, as it diminishes the importance of their electoral votes. Florida weighed adopting the approach in 1992, but ultimately rejected the idea out of concern that candidates would pay less attention to the Sunshine State if they were competing for only a share of its electoral votes as opposed to the entire bloc.

Second, while the district plan might be attractive if our congressional districts were drawn along coherent democratic lines, they are not. Hyperpartisan gerrymandering has utterly distorted the ability of congressional districts to accurately reflect the realities of party support in America. Consider the special election that Alabama held in 2017 to fill the Senate seat left vacant when Jeff Sessions took over as U.S. attorney general. Democrat Doug Jones defeated Republican Roy Moore, an unusual outcome in this deeply red state—and did so despite winning only one of Alabama's seven congressional districts.[13] This anomalous result was the direct consequence of GOP gerrymandering, which packed a large concentration of the state's African American voters into a single congressional district while distributing the remaining black voters around six white-majority districts. Adopting the districtwide system would simply reify these distortions.[14]

The most intriguing effort at an end run around the Electoral

College is the National Popular Vote Interstate Compact (NPVIC) initiative, whereby states pledge their electoral votes to the national popular-vote winner rather than the state vote winner. If states controlling a majority of Electoral College votes sign on to the initiative, then our present system would effectively be amended—and so far, the initiative has gathered 196 electoral votes, bringing it within striking distance of the 270 that represent an electoral majority.

But the NPVIC is problematic on several counts. Securing the remaining votes will require classic swing states to sign on, precisely those states that most benefit from the outsized role they play under our current system. Second, the scheme will certainly invite constitutional challenge.[15] Finally, there is the ticklish matter of enforcing compliance. Imagine a tight national contest in which the popular vote in an NPVIC state went for the loser of the national vote. The state legislature is controlled by the party of the loser, and the national electoral outcome is so close that if our NPVIC state breaks ranks and casts its electoral votes in accord with its own state outcome, the loser will win and become president. In such a case, the temptation to defect would be overwhelming. It's not clear what could stop our NPVIC state from breaking ranks.[16]

One final defect with our present system of presidential election deserves mention. A winner-take-all system, whether at the district, state, or national level, makes it virtually impossible for third parties to prevail in a presidential race. Whether this is a good or bad thing can be debated. At the same time, the system allows third-party candidates to play a spoiler effect. And this is decidedly, *emphatically* bad. Recall the role that Ralph Nader played in the election of 2000. Had Nader not been in the race, Gore would have handily carried Florida—meaning no hanging chads, no *Bush v. Gore*, and arguably no Iraq War. By permitting third-party candidates to operate only as spoilers—that is, by peeling away votes from the most popular candidate—our system permits the likes of a George W. Bush to emerge as the plurality winner in a state in which most voters oppose him.

Other electoral systems, such as France's, control this "spoiler effect" by having a national runoff. A first round of elections identifies the two most popular candidates, who then alone face off in the second round. The virtue of such a system is that it eliminates a profoundly antidemocratic outcome—the election of a plurality winner who is in effect not the most popular candidate. Our system permits and even invites such an outcome.[17]

Admittedly, the Electoral College has its defenders. By empowering the states, and not the people, to elect the president, it is said to promote federalism—the principle, undergirding the architecture of the Constitution, that distributes power between the states and Washington. The Electoral College is also said to act against regionalism, by ensuring that a candidate cannot capture the White House simply by appealing to supermajorities on, say, the coasts.

The problem with these defenses is that they have nothing to do with the original rationale for the system, but rather take the form of post hoc justifications for a mechanism that long ago lost its animating logic. More to the point, none can remotely justify the truly antidemocratic outcomes that result from the system's periodic misfires.

In other words, even if we assume, perhaps naively, that the 2020 election unfolds *without* fraud, voter suppression, hacking, foreign interference, or disinformation campaigns, it is still possible that Trump will win reelection without ever coming close to commanding a popular-vote majority. The peculiarities of the Electoral College could well hand him the 270 votes necessary for a win—again.

And yet the Electoral College is more than simply anachronistic, opaque, and prone to subverting the people's will. It is also capable of producing something more troubling than a bad result—it may produce no clear result at all, which was the case not only in

2000 but also in 1800 and 1876. And a murky or confusing result is immeasurably worse than one in which the popular-vote loser wins. The latter may be antidemocratic but is not destabilizing per se. A confusing result, by contrast, invites political discord. As we shall see, the fact that we managed to avoid such electoral meltdowns in 1800, 1876, and 2000 had less to do with the processes in place than it did with the character of those seeking higher office. Slot Donald Trump in the place of Samuel Tilden in 1876, or Al Gore in 2000, and you have a constitutional crisis with no clear exit.

CHAPTER 12

A Constitutional Anachronism

In the Hollywood classic *Mr. Smith Goes to Washington*, the idealistic young senator played by Jimmy Stewart reads aloud from a hefty tome as he launches his valiant filibuster against a corrupt appropriations bill. At some point, we catch a glimpse of the thick book from which Senator Smith reads—the U.S. Constitution. But anyone familiar with our Constitution knows there's something wrong with the scene. The Constitution is short. The original document drafted in Philadelphia in the steamy summer of 1787 had roughly forty-five hundred words—the length of a typical *New Yorker* story.

Readers of the Constitution also know that it begins with the words "We the People of the United States, in Order to form a more perfect Union..." The words "more perfect Union" remind us that this was not the nation's first stab at designing a Constitution. Ratified in 1781, the Articles of Confederation created a less than perfect union. Among other problems, the Articles lacked any chief executive capable of executing the law or acting as commander in chief.

The Philadelphia convention sought to correct this defect. In creating an executive branch with power concentrated in the hands of a single president, the delegates had to decide how the nation's chief executive would be chosen. A good deal of time was spent discussing this matter, with debate divided between those who supported giving Congress the power to elect the president, and those, such as James Madison, who supported direct election.

Both proposals invited strong objections. Giving Congress the power to elect the president would, it was feared, leave the chief executive overly beholden to the legislative branch. Direct election, by contrast, was opposed by the southern states. As the white voting population of these states was small relative to their entire population, direct election would dilute the power of citizens of slave states to choose the nation's chief executive.[1]

Also decisive was the fear that voters in a national election would prove incapable of making an informed choice about the candidates. The original thirteen states represented a substantial landmass and national news traveled slowly, if at all. How would voters be able to decide among candidates about whom they knew nothing? Delegate Elbridge Gerry, who decades later as governor of Massachusetts would carve a congressional district into the shape of a salamander and so bequeath us the term "gerrymander," warned of the "ignorance of the people," fearing they would be "too little informed of personal characteristics in larger districts and liable of deceptions."[2] Roger Sherman echoed this concern: "The people 'will never be sufficiently informed of characters' to make a choice."[3]

And so James Wilson, a delegate from Pennsylvania who originally endorsed direct election, offered a compromise in the form of an Electoral College. Electors would be persons of higher political standing, capable of exercising informed choice and reasoned deliberation—that is to say, prominent educated white men. In *Federalist* No. 68, Alexander Hamilton, a strong supporter of Wilson's proposal, argued that entrusting the task to such men "affords a moral certainty, that the office of President will never fall to the lot of any man who is not in an eminent degree endowed with the

requisite qualifications."[4] Not everyone shared Hamilton's enthusiasm. But Wilson's compromise came late in the day, and without
a great deal of debate or deliberation it gained acceptance as "the
second choice of many delegates though the first choice of few."[5]

As to how these men of discernment were to be chosen, the Constitution leaves the matter entirely in the hands of the legislature of each
state, to be decided "in such Manner as the Legislature thereof may
direct."[6] Early presidential elections witnessed the direct appointment
of electors by state legislatures, but the practice quickly devolved as
states began experimenting with different methods of selecting their
electors. Some retained direct legislative appointment, while others
moved to a statewide popular vote. With more and more states adopting the more democratic approach, 1824 marked the first presidential
election for which we have a record of the national popular vote.[7] And
while some states briefly awarded electors based on the district winner, the statewide winner-take-all approach, which increased a state's
power to influence the national outcome, soon became the norm.
By 1832, South Carolina remained the only state to rely on direct
appointment, a practice it didn't abandon until 1861.[8]

Once states vested the selection of electors in the hands of the
people, the original rationale for the unusual system—choosing persons of independent judgment—was gone. As early as 1816, Rufus
King, who had been a delegate to the Philadelphia constitutional
convention, lamented that the election of the president "is no longer
the process that the Constitution contemplated." Electors, King rue-
fully observed, now functioned as "mere . . . toys that nod when . . . set
in motion."[9] And that is the system we still have today. As Supreme
Court justice Robert Jackson put it, electors are "party lackeys and
intellectual nonentities to whose memory we might just paraphrase
a tuneful satire: They always voted at their Party's call / And never
thought of thinking for themselves at all."[10]

Today, most people would say that is how electors *should* act—a fact that reminds us just how far the Electoral College has wandered from its original logic. To put it differently, none of the original justifications for the Electoral College remain persuasive or relevant. We keep it in place not because we believe that the system is wise or efficient but simply because change is virtually impossible. And so every four years we go to the polls, hoping that a badly anachronistic system won't produce the antidemocratic result of a president who loses the national popular vote—or worse.

CHAPTER 13

Catastrophe No. 1

Faithlessness

What does worse look like?

For one answer, let's recall the 2000 election, in which George W. Bush received 271 Electoral College votes, one more than a bare majority, and Al Gore received 266. This left one vote unaccounted for. It belonged to Barbara Lett-Simmons, an elector from Washington, D.C., pledged to Gore, who abstained from voting in protest against the District's lack of representation in the House of Representatives. Lett-Simmons was what is known as a "faithless elector"—an elector who either abstains from voting or votes for a candidate other than the one to whom they were pledged. Lett-Simmons called her act one of civil disobedience and not faithlessness, noting that she would have voted for Gore, who easily carried D.C., had the outcome been in the balance.

Scholars have documented 167 cases of electors voting faithlessly in our history—typically, as in the case of Lett-Simmons, to make a symbolic statement. In 1956, a Democratic elector in Alabama pledged to Adlai Stevenson instead voted for a local circuit judge, with the declaration, "I have fulfilled my obligations to the people of Alabama. I'm talking about the white people."[1] In 2016, a Democratic elector in Washington State pledged to Hillary Clinton voted for Faith Spotted Eagle, a prominent Native American activist.

To date, none of the instances of electors breaking ranks have affected the outcome of an election. But there is nothing to say they cannot. Indeed, in an extremely tight election, the incentives to do so rise dramatically. Missouri senator Thomas Hart Benton long ago warned of the danger of an elector giving or selling his vote to the "adverse candidate," in "violation of all the pledges that have been taken of him." The act "is easily committed," Benton warned, adding that "detection is difficult; . . . [and] the injury irreparable."[2]

With that in mind, let's return to the 2020 election and imagine that on Wednesday morning, November 4, results indicate that despite receiving five million fewer votes than Joe Biden, President Trump has won reelection, garnering 271 electoral votes to Biden's 267. The president celebrates his historic victory in a triumphant tweet: "Winning the popular vote is easy, winning the electoral college is HARD! They said it couldn't be done TWICE. But the PEOPLE in their WISDOM LOVE Trump!! KAGA!!"

Things are looking good for the president—that is, until December 14, 2020, when electors across the nation meet in their respective state capitals and officially cast their votes. The balloting proceeds as anticipated—except in Pennsylvania. The Pennsylvania contest was among the tightest in the country, with Trump prevailing by fifteen thousand votes, capturing the state's hefty prize of twenty electoral votes and effectively securing his victory over Biden. Only now something extraordinary happens in the Pennsylvania State Capitol in Harrisburg. Despite the best efforts of the Trump campaign to draw the party's electors from the most faithful and diehard Trumpians, two Republican electors unexpectedly break ranks. In an interview later that day, one elector explains, "I am pledged to the GOP, not to President Trump. I can no longer abide by Mr. Trump's politics of destruction. I have therefore cast my vote for Mitt Romney." A second Republican elector follows suit, issuing a similar statement. "I cannot in good conscience stand with this president. I have joined my colleague in voting for Senator Romney. Long live the GOP."

These defections leave Trump with 269 electoral votes, one short of a constitutionally required majority. The nation struggles to absorb the meaning of what has happened, and yet the Constitution is clear on the matter: If no candidate has an Electoral College majority, the matter moves to the House of Representatives. As it did in 1800 and 1824, the House will elect the next president.

Chaos erupts. The president unleashes a Twitterstorm coarse even by his standards. "BULLSHIT rains [sic] in PA!!! TREASON-OUS 'electors' trying to DEFRAUD the American People. They won't get away with this UNCONSTITUTIONAL fraud!" More ominously, Trump ends a second tweet with a simple declaration: "I AM the president for the next four years."

Right-wing media echo Trump's insistence that the two electors have acted in an unconstitutional and even criminal fashion. By contrast, in the pages of the *New York Times* and the *Washington Post*, legal pundits opine that the Constitution vests electors with the right to cast their vote for whomever they choose. Some, including such prominent conservatives as George Will, note that in voting for Romney, the two "faithless" electors exercised their own independent judgment—that is, they acted in precisely the manner that framers such as Hamilton intended. One pundit dubs the two electors the "Hamiltonian duo." Democrats hail them as national heroes. In a press conference, Nancy Pelosi objects to the "faithless" label; "by defending our Constitution against a dangerous demagogue who has placed himself above our law," she says, "the 'Hamiltonian duo' are keeping the faith." *Faithful not Faithless* bumper stickers appear on thousands of Subarus and Priuses on the East and West Coasts.

Who is correct? Have the two electors acted in blatant violation of the Constitution and perhaps the law? Or have they acted in accordance with a power granted them in the Constitution?

The incredible and rather disastrous answer is—*it's not clear.*

In recent decades, thirty-two states and the District of Columbia have passed laws against faithless electors. Some states require electors to take a formal oath pledging that they will bind themselves to the state's popular-vote winner, but impose no penalty for noncompliance. Others, such as New Mexico and South Carolina, have made a failure to vote as pledged a punishable crime—although the vote as cast still counts. Still others, such as Indiana and Minnesota, void and replace the votes of electors who don't cast their ballots in line with the state's popular-vote winner.[3]

The 2016 election directed a spotlight on Colorado, one of the states that binds electors. Hillary Clinton handily won Colorado, but three Democratic electors sought to vote for Ohio governor John Kasich as part of a long-shot effort to find a consensus alternative to Donald Trump. The Colorado secretary of state ordered the three to cast their votes as state law required or face replacement (the Colorado statute did not mandate replacement, but the secretary defended his action as necessary to enforce the law). Two of the electors complied, while the third, Michael Baca, at the time a twenty-four-year-old graduate student, refused, and found himself replaced by a Democratic elector, who then dutifully cast his vote for Clinton.

Mr. Baca filed suit, and in August 2019, a divided three-judge panel of the 10th Circuit Court of Appeals in Denver issued a potentially landmark ruling.[4] In a 125-page opinion, the court held that the state secretary had "impermissibly interfered with Mr. Baca's exercise of his right to vote as a presidential elector." In ordering Baca's removal, the secretary had "acted unconstitutionally." The court concluded, "Electors, once appointed, are free to vote as they choose."[5]

If taken as the final word on the matter, the court's decision suggests that state laws constraining faithless electors are unconstitutional. And yet barely three months earlier, in May 2019, the Washington State Supreme Court reached the opposite conclusion, holding that a state can use its criminal law to enforce electoral pledges.[6]

Which court is correct? Alas, we don't know, because the Supreme Court has never decided on the matter.[7] The closest it has come was in 1952, when it concluded that a state may rightfully exclude, or allow political parties to exclude, electors who refuse to pledge support for their parties' nominees.[8] But that holding involved the pre-election pledging of electors, not electors who prove faithless afterward. Even then, the five-person majority opinion elicited a powerful dissent from Justice Jackson, who argued that "no one faithful to our history can deny that the plan originally contemplated...that electors would be free agents, to exercise an independent and nonpartisan judgment as to the men best qualified for the Nation's highest offices."[9]

Things should be clearer by the time of the 2020 election, as the Supreme Court has recently decided to review the Colorado and Washington cases, with a decision due in June 2020—four months before the election. How will the Court decide? Originalists, such as Clarence Thomas, will presumably agree with the 10th Circuit that the Constitution gives electors deliberative freedom.[10] Still, the issue does not divide along clear ideological lines and so resists easy prognostication.

But let us assume for the moment that the Supreme Court

upholds the constitutionality of state laws that penalize and/or replace faithless electors. In siding with Washington State and setting aside the opinion of the 10th Circuit, would the Court's ruling defuse the rapidly escalating electoral crisis?

I think not. For one thing, eighteen states do not bind their electors—and Pennsylvania is one of them. So let us return to Harrisburg. The Pennsylvania state legislature is controlled by Republicans who support the president. In an emergency session, and over the strenuous objections of state Democrats, they vote to cancel the electoral ballots of the two Romney electors and replace them with two party faithfuls who promptly vote for Trump. State Republicans declare they are simply acting consistent with the Supreme Court's June 2020 ruling. Trump ecstatically tweets, "The COUP has FAILED!!! I AM the ONCE AND FUTURE PRESIDENT!!"

State Democrats are apoplectic. While the Supreme Court, they argue, upheld the right of states to pass laws regulating faithless electors, Pennsylvania has no such law. Having failed to pass a law before the election, the state assembly cannot simply act in an ex post facto manner to alter a result the Republican majority doesn't like.

Jack Balkin of Yale Law School has observed that the "central task of constitutions is to keep disagreement within the bounds of ordinary politics rather than breaking down into anarchy, violence, or civil war."[11] When they fail at this task, we find ourselves in a constitutional crisis. This is precisely the situation that the nation now confronts.

Lawmakers in both parties mobilize. Recall that according to federal law, the governor of every state is required to send the certified vote of the electors by registered mail to the president of the Senate, where it will be opened and counted on January 6, 2021. The governor of Pennsylvania, Tom Wolf, is a Democrat. Anticipating that the Republican-led state legislature would try to void the votes for Romney, Wolf certifies the vote awarding eighteen votes to Trump and two to Romney and mails this certificate on to Congress.

State Republicans, however, have anticipated Governor Wolf's move. Having voted to void the ballots cast for Romney and having replaced the two faithless electors with Trump supporters, the legislature now approves its own certificate, awarding all twenty Electoral College votes to Trump. That, too, goes off by certified mail to Congress.

It is 1:00 p.m. on January 6, 2021. The joint session has gathered in the House chambers. Vice President Pence, the president of the Senate, gavels the Congress into session. In alphabetical order, Pence opens and presents the mailed certificates of the states and the District of Columbia. "Tellers"—two members of the House and the Senate, appointed in advance—dutifully read the certificates, and record and count the votes. In most elections, this is a pro forma exercise; in 2013, the joint session lasted a total of twenty-three minutes.[12]

But not this year. The chamber is already abuzz after Oregon's votes have been announced. Moving on alphabetically, Vice President Pence announces, "The chair hands to the teller the certificates of the electors for president and vice president for the state of Pennsylvania." *Certificates*? Pennsylvania has submitted two different certified sets of electoral votes.

Impossible, you say? And yet such a scenario has already occurred in our history—and it nearly tore the nation apart.

The year was 1876. The presidential race pitted the Republican governor of Ohio, Rutherford B. Hayes, against the Democratic governor of New York, Samuel Tilden. With over 80 percent of eligible voters casting ballots—the highest percentage in American history—Tilden scored a solid victory in the national popular vote, beating Hayes by roughly 3 percent of votes cast. He also appeared set to secure an Electoral College victory: With 185 votes

representing an electoral majority at the time, Tilden had clearly
secured 184 votes to Hayes's 165. And while the results in Florida,
Louisiana, and South Carolina were close, Tilden appeared also to
have carried these states and their remaining twenty electoral votes.[13]

Republicans, however, still controlled the machinery of Reconstruction governments in those three states, and received a stern direc-
tive from the national GOP to "hold their state."[14] If Republicans in
these states could swing all twenty votes over to Hayes, then he, and
not Tilden, would become the next president. With their marching
orders, local Republicans worked to manipulate the vote in the three
states. In Florida, the shenanigans of a Republican-led canvassing
board resulted in a fresh count that gave Hayes the state by 924 votes.
Republicans engineered similar outcomes in South Carolina and Louisiana, and Republican governors in these states happily certified the
results, awarding Hayes all twenty outstanding electoral votes.

State Democrats were not about to sit idly by while the election
was stolen out from under them, especially given the fact that Tilden needed just a single remaining electoral vote to secure the presidency. In Florida, Tilden's electors met, cast their ballots, and the
state attorney general, a Democrat, certified their result and sent it
on to Congress. In the case of South Carolina, Tilden's electors sent
their own certified result directly to D.C.[15]

And so at the joint session, Congress found itself confronted
with two sets of certified returns from each of three states. Decades
earlier, Joseph Story, the great Supreme Court justice and expositor
of constitutional history, had noted that the Constitution provided
no guidance should a controversy arise "as to the regularity and
authenticity of the returns of the electoral votes." The framers, Story
worried, seemed "to have taken for granted that nothing more was
necessary, than to open the certificates...in the presence of both
houses, and to count the names and numbers."[16]

Story's worry now proved prescient. Confronted with conflicting certificates, Congress found itself at an impasse. Democrats controlled the House of Representatives, Republicans the Senate. Unable to work its way out of the deadlock, Congress agreed to a one-off statutory fix. Lawmakers created an electoral commission "whose authority," as one congressman put it, "none can question and whose decision all will accept as final."[17] The fifteen-person commission was to include five senators, five members of the House, and five members of the Supreme Court. Predictably, the matter of party membership proved highly contentious. The selected congressmen were equally split between Republicans and Democrats, while two justices drawn from the Supreme Court were thought to lean Republican and two Democratic. With the commission equally divided seven to seven along party lines, the tiebreaker would be David Davis, a Supreme Court justice famous for his fierce independence.[18]

And yet Davis would never end up serving. In what has been called "one of the greatest blunders in American political history,"[19] Illinois's Democrat-controlled legislature chose this inopportune moment to name Justice Davis to a vacancy in the U.S. Senate. With Davis now unable to serve, a replacement had to be found from the ranks of the Supreme Court.[20] Alas, finding a second, equally nonpartisan justice proved impossible. Chosen was Joseph Bradley—nominated to the Supreme Court by President Ulysses S. Grant—who decisively sided with the Republican faction. Bradley cast the tiebreaking vote in awarding Hayes all twenty electoral votes, and with them, the narrowest of Electoral College victories, 185–184.

Congressional Democrats, dismayed with the outcome, contemplated filibustering to delay Congress from authorizing the commission's results. If no candidate received an Electoral College majority, the election would move to the House, which was controlled by the Democrats. With no resolution in sight, the nation watched with dread the approach of March 4, 1877, inauguration day.[21] A settlement appeared to be reached on March 2. In a secret deal with southern Democrats, Hayes and leading Republicans agreed to remove the remaining federal troops from the South, effectively ending Reconstruction. In return, Tilden instructed Democratic congressmen to acquiesce to the completion of the electoral count.

Still, the situation remained volatile. With rumors flying that Tilden was planning his own separate inauguration in New York, President Grant weighed declaring martial law. The prospect of two political rivals both claiming to be the nation's lawful commander in chief, each with his own fervent supporters, terrified a nation still recovering from the convulsions of civil war. Fortunately, Tilden, along with several key Democratic statesmen, was not willing to push the country past the brink; instead, Tilden placed the nation's good ahead of his personal political fortunes.

But the resolution of the electoral crisis of 1876 can hardly be called happy. It would be more appropriate to say that catastrophe was avoided by disaster. By agreeing to end Reconstruction as the price for Hayes's election, Republicans gave southern Democrats the freedom to construct an apartheid South engineered through Jim Crow laws and enforced by acts of terror. A constitutional truce between Republicans and Democrats was negotiated over the heads—and on the backs—of America's black citizens.

————

Before we return to the crisis unfolding in Congress on January 6, 2021, we need to linger a bit longer in the late nineteenth century. In the wake of the Hayes-Tilden near-fiasco, lawmakers felt a pressing need to guard against any future repeats. They weighed drafting a constitutional amendment that would create a dedicated independent tribunal tasked with solving electoral controversies. But the unhappy experience with the Hayes-Tilden commission eroded support for such a constitutional fix. The controversial role that Justice Bradley had played in 1877 also soured lawmakers on vesting the power of resolution in the Supreme Court.

And so Congress struggled with the problem for a decade before finally framing a grossly deficient statutory solution. The Electoral Count Act of 1887 (ECA)[22]—still on the books and operative— dictates a series of rules and procedures meant to guide Congress should a controversy ever again arise over a state's Electoral College votes. That, in any case, was the idea, but not the execution. A contemporaneous expositor described the law as "very confused, almost unintelligible."[23] One present-day expert calls it "convoluted" and "essentially incomprehensible,"[24] while another deems it "inadequate...and arguably unconstitutional."[25] Not only does it fail to anticipate several destabilizing contingencies, but the plans it does put in place are so confusing as to invite controversy rather than settle it. In 2000, when the ECA threatened to kick in, jurists and commentators were unable to agree about the meaning of even its most basic provisions.[26]

Given the glaring deficiencies of the law, the nation can count itself lucky that it has not faced a repeat of the Hayes-Tilden disaster. The first and only time that the provisions of the ECA were triggered came in 1969, and the results were not promising. In 1968, Richard Nixon carried North Carolina, but a faithless Republican elector cast his vote for George Wallace, the southern segregationist who had run as a third-party candidate. North Carolina's governor duly certified the state result, including the single vote for Wallace, and forwarded it to Congress. During the subsequent joint session, members of both the House and the Senate challenged the vote for Wallace.[27] Suddenly lawmakers had to make sense of one of the ECA's characteristically opaque passages. According to the law:

> No electoral vote or votes from any state which shall have
> been regularly given by electors whose appointment has been
> lawfully certified...shall be rejected, but the two Houses
> concurrently may reject the vote or votes when they agree that
> such vote or votes have not been so regularly given by electors
> whose appointment has been so certified.[28]

What does this semantic salad mean? It appears that Congress
must accept "regularly given" Electoral College votes—unless it
decides not to. As to what constitutes a "regularly given" electoral
vote, the law is silent.

If the ECA conspicuously fails to tell Congress how to resolve
controversies, it at least tells them how to try—instructing both
houses to debate the matter separately under strict time constraints.
Members may speak only once and for no more than five minutes;
debate must end after two hours.

In 1969, the chambers duly divided and debated the matter. But
with no instruction as to the meaning of a "regularly given" electoral
vote, some members of Congress argued that the vote for Wallace was
not regularly given, while others insisted that it was. Following the
procedure outlined in the ECA, both houses then voted, with both
narrowly rejecting the objections to counting the rogue vote.[29] And
so Nixon ended up with 301 Electoral College votes, and not 302.
Nothing turned on the outcome. The debate was entirely academic.

Not so in our 2021 scenario. Here, unsurprisingly, Republican
lawmakers in both the House and Senate challenge the two break-
away votes from Pennsylvania as "not regularly given," while their
Democratic counterparts raise the identical challenge to the two
"replacement" votes certified by the state assembly. The two bodies
separate, and debate quickly turns acrimonious. Both sides appeal to
the Supreme Court's decision of June 2020, only to reach opposite

conclusions. Republicans insist the Court's ruling means the faithless electors were not "regularly given"; Democrats insist that because Pennsylvania had no law in place concerning faithless electors, the votes were "regularly given." The Supreme Court refuses to intervene, leaving the interpretation of the ECA up to Congress itself. Time limits fall by the wayside, and not until the early hours of January 7 do the two houses vote on the challenges.

The results are predictable: The Republican-controlled Senate votes to reject the votes of Pennsylvania's two "faithless" electors and to count the substitute votes instead, while the House, controlled by Democrats, does exactly the opposite, voting to reject the challenge to the "Hamiltonian" electors and to support the challenge to the substitute votes.

What now? This is not 1876 or 1968 or 2000. Now we have an incumbent with a twitchy Twitter finger more than happy to play constitutional brinkmanship. The same coalition that shot down the effort to remove Trump from office rallies behind the president, embracing and powerfully amplifying his charges of fraud and Deep State conspiracies. Trump urges his vociferous supporters—millions of whom are armed—to resist.

A complete electoral meltdown threatens. Congress remains in session, but the hostility and distrust between the parties dooms any effort at a solution.

And now a further defect of the ECA comes to the fore. The 1887 law fails to make clear who actually gets to count the electoral results:

> If more than one return or paper purporting to be a return from a State shall have been received by the President of the Senate, those votes, and those only, shall be counted which shall have been regularly given.[30]

There again is that bugaboo—"regularly given." And what about "shall be counted"—yes, but by whom? Seizing on the language that precedes this passive construction, congressional Republicans now insist that it is the president of the Senate who gets to make the determinative count—that is, Vice President Pence. Pence obviously supports the votes submitted by the Pennsylvania assembly awarding Trump all twenty of the state's votes.

Democrats scream bloody murder. They argue that the law grants the president of the Senate only a ceremonial, not a substantive role. Given Pence's vested role in the administration of one of the two candidates, it would be nothing short of grotesque to give him the power to decide which votes have been "regularly given." If anything, the ECA privileges votes certified by a state's governor. The houses remain deadlocked.

The matter is appealed to the Supreme Court, but the Court is reluctant to intervene, again insisting that the interpretation of the ECA is up to Congress itself. Moreover, many legal experts observe that by the terms of the ECA, once an election controversy reaches Congress, the Court no longer has jurisdiction over the matter— Congress and Congress alone has authority to resolve the crisis.

If it only could. It is now January 13, one week before the inauguration. Some lawmakers propose simply striking the two votes in question. Neither Trump nor Romney will get them. But this proposal raises more questions than it answers. Not counting the votes would still leave Trump with only 269 electoral votes and Biden with 267. The Constitution requires a victor to receive a majority of votes. If the two are struck, are they also struck from the total needed to win? If so, then only 536 and not 538 votes are up for grabs, and Trump would be the winner. If not, then neither candidate has received an electoral majority—and the House assumes the responsibility for electing the next president.

Republicans insist that striking the electors changes both the numerator *and* the denominator, while Democrats argue that it changes only the numerator, leaving the denominator unchanged. What does the ECA say?

In the law's most glaring omission, *it says nothing at all.*

The law simply says one must receive a "majority of votes from all electors authoritatively appointed." And because it fails to define "authoritatively appointed," it provides no guidance whatsoever about the consequence of striking electoral votes. Congress remains at an impasse.

Meanwhile, Trump's tweets assume an apocalyptic tone. "CIVIL WAR will erupt," he tweets, "if the CORRUPT Dems and Deep-State Trump Haters try to CHEAT me out of office!!!!"

Three days before the scheduled inauguration, things suddenly change in the Senate. Recall that when Trump was impeached by the House, a supermajority in the Senate would have had to vote for his removal. The present challenges to the Pennsylvania votes, however, can be resolved by simple majorities in each chamber. All along, Mitt Romney has voted with Senate Democrats. Now, on January 17, he is suddenly joined by three moderate Republicans, who cite the urgency of preserving the fundamental constitutional order of governance. Congress holds a fresh vote. This time both the House and the Senate—the latter by 51 to 49—accept the certificate submitted by Pennsylvania's governor.

At last all 538 electoral votes have been accounted for. The final tally: Trump 269, Biden 267, and Romney 2. For the first time since 1824, the House of Representatives will elect the next president. And yet the outcome in the House, despite the solid Democratic majority there, is hardly a foregone conclusion. By the terms of our beloved but badly antiquated Constitution, when an election lands in the House, each individual House member does not get to cast a vote; rather, *each state delegation* has but a single vote. Wyoming has as much say as California in electing the president. And while Democrats presently enjoy a firm House majority, with 235 seats to the Republicans' 199 (with one seat vacant), the tally of individual state delegations tells a different story. Republicans currently have majority delegations in twenty-six states to the Democrats' twenty-three, with one state evenly split. By the procedures set forth in the Constitution, the House as currently constituted would reelect Trump.

Only the House constituted by the 2018 midterms is not the body that now must decide the 2020 election. That decision falls to the newly elected 117th Congress, voted in on November 3, 2020. Although our crystal ball is hard to read, let us assume that Democrats make modest gains in 2020: They pick up one seat in Pennsylvania, which at present is evenly split between the two parties; and two seats in Wisconsin, making them the majority delegation there as well. Now, although the overall composition of the House remains firmly in the hands of Democrats, state delegations are evenly split between Democrats and Republicans. And that even split again paralyzes the effort to elect the next president.

January 20 looms with no resolution in sight. The Twentieth Amendment says, "If a President shall not have been chosen before the time fixed for the beginning of his term, or if the President elect shall have failed to qualify, then the Vice President elect shall act as President until a President shall have qualified."

But do we have a vice president? Just as the Constitution vests the House with the power to elect the next president, it hands the power to elect the vice president to the Senate. Republicans currently enjoy a majority in the Senate, but let's assume that Democrats have gained one seat in the 2020 senatorial races. With Romney and, say, one other moderate Republican refusing to support Pence, the chamber's vote is evenly divided 50–50. The Twelfth Amendment states that to be elected, the vice president must win a "majority of the whole number" of senators. This language appears clear, but is it?

Typically, when the Senate is evenly split, the president of the Senate casts the tiebreaking vote. The president of the Senate, however, remains Vice President Pence. Does the Constitution permit Pence to cast the vote that would make him the acting president? Or does a "majority of the whole number" of senators mean that senators *alone* may participate in the vote?

Again, the Constitution offers no guidance. At this point, and despite its ongoing reluctance, the Supreme Court steps into the fray, holding that the Constitution's language means that only senators may participate in the vote. And so, come noon on January 20, we have neither a president nor a vice president.

Federal law does, mercifully, anticipate such a scenario. In this case, the presidency devolves to the Speaker of the House.[31] As of 12:01 a.m. EST on January 20, 2021, Nancy Pelosi is acting president of the United States.

Not, however, according to Donald Trump, who remains hunkered down in the White House, vowing to stay there. "I will FIGHT to DEFEND our GREAT DEMOCRACY!!" he tweets, and announces he will do what Samuel Tilden was rumored to have contemplated in 1877—he will stage his own inauguration. The nation's capital witnesses a chaotic scene. No sooner has Chief Justice John Roberts sworn in Nancy Pelosi as acting president than Trump is sworn in on the South Lawn of the White House. Administering the oath of office is Justice Clarence Thomas.

Trump then orders Attorney General Barr to notify the heads of the military that he remains commander in chief, in control of the nation's nuclear codes. Barr meanwhile receives word from Pelosi that according to the clear dictates of the Constitution, she is now commander in chief, and she instructs him to notify the military of this fact. Should Barr decline to do so, he will promptly be replaced by an acting attorney general willing to execute her order. Trump immediately countermands Pelosi's order by tweet: "I AM COMMANDER IN CHIEF. I WILL CRUSH THIS COUP BY THE PELOSI GANG AND THE TREASONOUS DEMOCRATS!!!"

Before you accuse me of conjuring a bizarre doomsday scenario better suited to a Netflix miniseries than a work of serious political analysis, recall how we got here. We imagined an extremely close outcome in 2020, an entirely plausible result and one the nation has experienced in the past. We further imagined that just two electors in a pivotal swing state choose to act "faithlessly"—again, surely possible. Finally, we imagined that as a consequence, that state ends up sending two different electoral certificates to Congress. It has happened before and could well happen again.

Into this mix we have added a wild card—a president who, in sharp contrast with his predecessors, places his personal brand above the nation's well-being, shows no regard for the norms of constitutional governance, and who, by defaming the electoral process and spreading meta-lies about the free press, has prepared his fervent supporters to distrust every voice other than his own. Throw in the extreme partisanship not seen in our national politics in decades, and the result is a constitutional crisis from which there is no clear exit.

Every worst-case scenario presents a kind of perfect storm, and what has made our scenario so explosive is not Trump's behavior alone: Congressional Republicans and the right-wing media aggressively support the president's defiance. And failures in constitutional design and gaps in the fabric of federal law work together to turn a crisis into a catastrophe. These flaws are not new. They emerged in dramatic fashion in 1876, and the effort to fix them failed. Luck and decency prevented these defects from causing a disaster in 2000. But in 2020 we have no Al Gore to save us from a complete electoral meltdown and the unrest and violence it could unleash. In this meltdown, we find to our dismay that the tools meant to defuse crises—our constitutional and legal processes—work only to make the meltdown inescapable. And once we find ourselves in this mess, nothing in our law or Constitution tells us how to walk it back.

CHAPTER 14

Catastrophe No. 2
Hack Attack

Our second crisis scenario turns our attention from Pennsylvania to another swing state, Michigan. It is November 3, and voter turnout is heavy statewide. Only something is very wrong in Detroit. Twenty minutes after polls open at 7:00 a.m. EST, Detroit is hit by a massive power failure, knocking out electricity to almost all of the city's 673,000 residents.[1] Utility workers at Detroit Energy struggle to identify the source of the problem. It is not until 2:00 p.m. that power is restored to some locations, but rolling blackouts continue to plague much of the city.

In those areas where power is restored, a fresh problem emerges. Widespread computer glitches prevent election officials from accessing lists of registered voters. As we shall see in the next chapter, provisional ballots may be used in such circumstances, but many polling stations find themselves lacking such ballots, and officials at those that have them haven't been properly trained to deal with the magnitude of the problem. When polls close at 8:00 p.m., polling stations throughout the city remain either without power or unable to access voting rolls.

At midnight and notwithstanding the reports of the mess coming from Detroit, major networks announce Trump's reelection. The final result is extremely close—in fact, Michigan's sixteen electoral votes account for Trump's winning margin of 280 to Biden's 265. As in 2016, Trump's victory in Michigan is narrow; around thirty thousand votes separate the two candidates. But has he in fact carried Michigan?

It is not until 4:00 a.m. on Wednesday, November 4, that Detroit Energy succeeds at restoring power to all locations in the city—and later that morning, election officials estimate that as a result of the disruptions, as many as 350,000 people in Detroit and outlying areas were prevented from casting their ballots. That number would appear to be pivotal. In 2016, 750,000 Americans voted in Michigan's Wayne County, which includes Detroit, with Hillary Clinton trouncing Trump there by close to 300,000 votes (520,000 votes to 230,000).[2] Now, in 2020, with the depletion caused by the power outage and computer glitches, Wayne County accounts for only 400,000 of the votes cast in Michigan.

At a noon press conference in front of city hall, Detroit mayor Mike Duggan acknowledges that the cause of the multiple failures remains unclear. "We're looking into anything and everything—including the possibility that our electrical grid and registration databases were hacked by a foreign adversary for the express purpose of disrupting voting in our city. But whatever the cause, it's clear that in the interests of a fair election we must and will conduct a revote in Wayne County."

———

How vulnerable is our national electoral system to such an event? The answer is that we do not *have* a national election system; our presidential contests are conducted in more than eight thousand distinct election jurisdictions.[3] On the one hand, this makes the task of hacking the election on a widespread basis extremely difficult, as launching a coordinated attack on so many distinct systems, with their different machines and methods, would be virtually impossible.[4]

But the bad news is that it's not necessary to disrupt the entire system in order to utterly disrupt a presidential election. This again is a vulnerability peculiar to the Electoral College, which, in the words of one expert, "creates a recurring incentive for strategic mischief," as one needs only to "suppress a relatively small number of votes to swing all of a state's electors."[5] Close elections will turn on the results in a handful of swing states, and so a targeted attack on those key states—or even a handful of districts within those states—can completely upend a national result. And an attack need not materially alter a result to be "successful"—it need only undermine confidence in the accuracy of the result.

So how vulnerable are the various systems in place across the United States? In Florida in 2000, antiquated equipment in Broward County and incompetently designed ballots in Palm Beach County cost Al Gore the presidency. The bits of paper that failed to dislodge from punched ballots—the notorious "hanging chads"—were produced by machines designed by IBM in the 1960s.[6] In the wake of the Florida debacle, Congress passed the Help America Vote Act of 2002 (HAVA), which, among other things, allocated money to states to replace out-of-date equipment and created a commission tasked with certifying the reliability of voting machines.[7]

But by 2016 many of those replacement machines had long needed replacing and were highly vulnerable to hackers. A report prepared by the Senate Intelligence Committee in 2019 concluded that Russian hackers targeted election systems *in all fifty states*, far more than the twenty-one attacks the government had previously reported. In

Illinois, Russian hackers penetrated the computer network of the state board of elections, gaining access to databases containing information on millions of registered voters. More alarming still, the report concluded that "Russian cyberactors were in a position to delete or change voter data."[8] In Florida, Russian hackers were likewise in a position to alter information in a county database.[9] Senator Marco Rubio expressed the concern of many when he imagined the "mass confusion" that would result if "on election day you go to vote and ... [your] voter registration information has been deleted from the systems."[10]

Despite possessing the capability to do so, the Russians apparently chose not to alter voter data in 2016, relying instead on a highly effective disinformation campaign. But the Senate report ominously suggests that Russia might have been exploring options "for use at a later date."[11] Since 2016, states have scrambled to improve the security of their electoral infrastructure, and while Congress has authorized hundreds of millions of dollars to aid these efforts, the sums still fall well short of the $2 billion that experts believe necessary to upgrade our various systems.[12]

More disturbing yet, we continue to lack mandatory national cybersecurity standards for the technology used in our elections. Other nations have not been so laggard. Confronted by a threat to its parliamentary election by Russian state hackers, Norway mandated the retention and counting of backup paper ballots for all computer-scanned ballots.[13] Experts agree that this kind of "voter-verified paper trail" provides the best prophylactic against electoral hacking.

And yet legislating such mandatory backups has been steadfastly resisted by congressional Republicans. In 2019, Senate majority leader Mitch McConnell held up an allocation of $250 million for state upgrades, charging that the allocation was part of a "highly partisan bill from the same folks who spent two years hyping up a conspiracy theory about President Trump and Russia."[14] Requiring computerized voting machines to produce a paper ballot, McConnell insisted, would constitute a federal intrusion in the local administration of elections.[15] While McConnell finally agreed to allocate the monies, congressional Republicans continue to reject the introduction of national election security standards. As Senator Ron Wyden, Democrat of Oregon, lamented, "There are not even any voluntary federal standards."[16]

Come the 2020 election, the share of voters who use machines that produce no paper trail, recently about one in four, will shrink to perhaps one in ten. That, of course, represents both a substantial improvement and a continuing, dramatic vulnerability. The 2018 midterms revealed Michigan—and Detroit specifically—as, in the words of an election expert, "one of the biggest problem areas."[17] And as Richard Clarke, formerly the nation's top counterterrorism official, has recently observed, a vulnerable electoral district could come under attack and never know it—as Clarke puts it, "they have no capability of knowing."[18] Simply realizing that a system has been breached requires a level of sophistication that many systems lack. Given the outsized role the Electoral College confers on swing states, the strength of our entire system of presidential elections is only as strong as its weakest link.

As our Detroit scenario imagines, the attack need not target the electoral system per se. Hackers could, for example, exploit vulnerabilities in the computer systems that control America's electrical grid. In 2015, Russian hackers attacked Ukraine's grid, causing widespread disruptions.[19] In 2018, the Cybersecurity and Infrastructure Security Agency within the Department of Homeland Security reported that Russian hackers had successfully penetrated parts of our electrical grid, and that they likely remain within it, capable of causing future disruptions.[20] Concentrate those disruptions on election day, and the result could be chaos.

Given the vulnerabilities of our electoral and electrical systems, we might at the very least hope that federal law details how to respond to election day emergencies. And yet, sadly it doesn't, again leaving things to the states. North Carolina, for example, grants emergency powers to the executive director of the state board of elections in the case of disruptions stemming from "a natural disaster, extremely inclement weather or armed conflict."[21] But it's far from clear that the disruption that plagues Detroit on November 3 even constitutes an emergency by this definition. In any case, Michigan remains one of the many states that lack any election emergency statute.

———

So let us return to Mayor Duggan's press conference on November 4, 2020, which ends with his call for a revote in Wayne County. This is not a recount. Recounts occur when problems emerge in the counting of votes or when the margin of victory is exceptionally small. In Detroit, however, there's nothing to recount. Democrats around the country immediately express support for Duggan's proposal. "We cannot reward foreign interference in our elections," Nancy Pelosi declares. "The only remedy is a revote."

Not surprisingly, the president promptly tweets his disagreement:

Mayor Duggan, a proven LOSER, is trying to hold others responsible for HIS CORRUPTION and INCOMPETENCE. Detroit has no one to blame but ITSELF! NO REVOTE!!

* * *

DETROIT doesn't get a revote because very LOW IQ mayor doesn't know how to HOLD AN ELECTION!! Every other city in AMERICA managed to vote, only Detroit FAILS. No revote for Dugan [*sic*] and his GARBAGE city!!

From a strategic standpoint, we can well appreciate the president's worries. Given his slender margin of victory in Michigan, a revote in Wayne County would virtually guarantee Biden enough votes to overcome Trump's statewide lead—and with Michigan's electoral votes in his ledger, Biden would be the next president of the United States. Trump's vociferous opposition is quickly taken up by congressional Republicans and the right-wing media. A fierce battle explodes over the legitimacy of a revote.

So what are the standards and protocols for staging a revote in a presidential election? The short answer, once again, is that there are none. As Norm Ornstein has observed, if a national election is disrupted, "We have no plan B.... There are no do-overs and no mechanism in place to ameliorate the effect."[22]

This is not to say that revotes haven't taken place. In 2002, Illinois officials ordered a do-over vote for a state house seat after learning that some ballots had been left uncounted, lost, or mistakenly cast by voters outside the district.[23] And earlier we observed that evidence of fraud in North Carolina's 9th Congressional District led the state board of elections to order a fresh contest. But no revote has ever been staged in a presidential contest. The North Carolina experience suggests why. There, the do-over vote was not completed until nearly a year after the midterms. While such a delay, and the vacancy it creates, may be acceptable in the case of a congressional seat, it would be intolerable in a presidential contest.

Still, federal law does seem to open the door to a revote. Without actually creating a provision for a revote, federal law holds that if a state "has held an election for the purpose of choosing electors, and has failed to make a choice on the date prescribed by law, the electors may be appointed on a subsequent day in such a manner as the legislature of such State may direct."[24] But has Michigan "failed to make a choice"?

Detroit insists the state has failed. Lawmakers in Lansing, the state capital, disagree. As in Pennsylvania, Republicans enjoy majorities in both houses of Michigan's state legislature, while the governor, Gretchen Whitmer, is a Democrat. State Republican lawmakers concede that the Detroit disruptions were "regrettable," but that Michigan has not "failed to make a choice." As the body empowered by federal law to order a subsequent vote, the legislature declares that it will not do so.

Detroit and the Biden campaign promptly file suit, asking a federal judge to order a fresh vote. Trump's lawyers demand the dismissal of the Democrats' suit; the Justice Department under William Barr's stewardship weighs in, arguing that the court must defer to the state legislature and that a revote would occasion chaos. Trump's team also argues that even if the court accepts that there was interference in the election, the interference came from abroad and not from anyone "acting under the color of state law." Consequently, the court is not authorized to order the extraordinary remedy that Detroit and Biden seek.[25]

Operating under intense political and time pressure, the district court orders a revote in Wayne County—"an unprecedented step," it rules, "made necessary to protect the very integrity of our democratic processes from an unprecedented attack."

President Trump condemns the decision. Reviving rhetoric he has used in the past, he blasts the "FAKE judge" as "a proven Trump hater" and threatens that "this OBAMA 'judge' will have to PAY!!"

Trump's lawyers and the Justice Department appeal directly to the Supreme Court, arguing that limiting the revote to Wayne County would violate the equal protection rights of voters in other parts of the state and country who were unable to vote as a result of unexpectedly long lines or defective election machines. While the Supreme Court relied on much the same argument in putting a halt to the targeted Florida recount in *Bush v. Gore*, now, with Chief

Justice Roberts delivering the surprise swing vote in a 5–4 ruling, the Court upholds Wayne County's revote order.

Frantic election officials in Wayne County scramble to organize the redo election. And yet a combination of inexperience and the need to ensure that the system cannot again be compromised results in several delays. Finally, the revote is set for Tuesday, December 8. The date is significant. We've already noted that federal law mandates that electors across the country meet in their state capitals on the Monday after the second Wednesday in December, which in 2020 falls on December 14.

But Michigan must actually settle its election six days earlier— by December 8. This is the so-called safe harbor date created by the Electoral Count Act of 1887. Eager to avoid a repeat of the Hays-Tilden nightmare, the framers of that law sought to encourage states to remedy their electoral disputes before they end up in Congress's lap. By the terms of the law, Congress will give the state's results "safe harbor"—that is, presumptive validity—provided the state has resolved all election-related messes *six days* before the electors physically gather.[26] Should a state miss this deadline, Congress is authorized to be far less deferential to the state's certification. By setting the election for December 8, officials in Detroit hope to have a clear result before the expiration of the safe harbor deadline.

In the days before the December 8 revote, Trump unleashes a Twitter barrage, urging his supporters to "BOYCOTT the FAKE 'election.'" Insisting that he has already won reelection and attacking the revote as the Democrats' "SECOND ILLEGAL IMPEACHMENT," he directs his base to sit out the "SHAM vote!"

The revote goes smoothly but the results dramatically confirm that Trump's supporters have followed his call. Biden receives nearly 280,000 votes, while the president gets a scant 15,000. Democrats declare that thanks to the Wayne County revote, Biden has now carried the state and so has been elected president. Trump and his supporters announce that they will not abide by the result; the lopsided outcome, they loudly insist, simply confirms that the redo was a total farce, a coup staged by corrupt Democrats.

In the statehouse in Lansing, the crisis escalates. Although the results of the revote are announced on the night of December 8, before the safe harbor deadline has passed, on December 14 the Republican-led majority in the state legislature announces that it will certify Trump's slate of electors based exclusively on the November 3 results. The legislature awards Trump all sixteen of Michigan's electoral college votes, effectively handing him the election.

Democratic governor Whitmer, meanwhile, appalled by the actions of the state's Republicans, announces on the same day that she has certified Biden's slate of electors, based on the combined results of November 3 and December 8. "It was the president who told his supporters not to participate in a perfectly fair revote," the governor declares. "That was his decision and he and his supporters must live with the consequences. The people of Michigan have spoken and I intend to heed their voice."

And so on January 6, 2021, Congress finds itself confronted with two electoral certificates from Michigan—much the same disaster we encountered in our first meltdown scenario.[27] Following the protocol we encountered in the last chapter, members of Congress raise objections to both certificates; the bodies debate the objections in their respective chambers, and reach the predictable result. The Senate, with its Republican majority, votes to accept the certificate for Trump submitted by the Michigan legislature, while the House, with its Democratic majority, votes to accept Governor Whitmer's certificate for Biden.

Lawmakers rage. Congressional Democrats insist that for once the ECA offers clear guidance. By its terms, "if the two Houses shall disagree" about which certificate to accept, "the votes of the electors whose appointment shall have been certified by the executive of the State, under the seal thereof, shall be counted."[28] Governor Whitmer is Michigan's executive, and so Congress must accept her certificate.

But congressional Republicans now insist that the language "shall be counted" is advisory, not legally binding. Supported by a number of legal scholars, they argue that the ECA would be unconstitutional if read to impose legally binding obligations on how Congress is to count electoral votes.[29]

Apoplectic Democrats file suit, petitioning the Supreme Court to direct Republicans to comply with the terms of the ECA. Alas, the hope that the Supreme Court can extricate us from this constitutional crisis turns out to be a pipe dream. For one thing, as we noted earlier, the drafters of the ECA specifically rejected tasking the Court with the resolution of such electoral disputes. As Senator John Sherman, a leading Republican lawmaker and statesman of the day, opined, "there is a feeling in this country that we ought not to mingle our great judicial tribunal with political questions."[30] Now, in 2020, the Court agrees, holding that it has no role to play in settling electoral questions once they reach Congress. It refuses to hear the Democrats' appeal, and the stalemate persists.

But let's assume a highly unlikely outcome: The Supreme Court does accept the case and, in another 5–4 decision with Chief Justice Roberts delivering the swing vote, decides that the ECA does indeed legally bind the Senate to accept Governor Whitmer's certificate. Will the crisis be resolved?

Hardly. No sooner has the Court announced its holding than the president tweets out a challenge: "John Roberts has made his decision. NOW LET HIM ENFORCE IT!!" The tweet pointedly echoes another instance of presidential defiance: In response to Chief Justice Marshall's recognition of the sovereignty rights of the

Cherokee nation in *Worcester v. Georgia* (1832), President Andrew Jackson is said to have quipped, "John Marshall has made his decision; now let him enforce it!" Even if apocryphal, Jackson's statement has come to bluntly underscore the fact that the Court has no actual power to enforce its rulings and instead must rely on the voluntary compliance of the coordinate branches of government.

Trump is hardly alone in rejecting the Court's opinion. Accusing the Court of overreach, congressional Republicans announce that they will not abide by the ruling. As members of the same institutional body that originally drafted and passed the ECA, these Republicans insist that their reading of the 1887 law has a deeper pedigree than the Court's.

The nation again finds itself in the grips of a constitutional crisis from which there is no clear exit. We need not rehearse in detail how the meltdown continues through January 20 and beyond—Congress paralyzed, Twitterstorms blasting from the White House, torrents of outrage cascading from cable television and talk radio, and violent threats sounding in all corners of the internet. To this toxic mix, let us add a coordinated disinformation campaign percolating through social media and orchestrated by a gleeful foreign adversary. And let us not forget that guns in this country remain in profuse supply and are largely concentrated in the hands of the president's most fervent, distrustful, and easily unsettled supporters. We are in for an unhappy time.

CHAPTER 15

Catastrophe No. 3
Big Blue Shift

Our third scenario brings three crucial swing states into play—Michigan, Wisconsin, and Pennsylvania. Trump carried all three in 2016, and their total of forty-six Electoral College votes gave him the presidency. Yet his margin of victory in these battleground states was exceptionally slim, a combined total of fewer than eighty thousand votes. Trump carried Michigan by fewer than eleven thousand votes, a 0.2 percent margin of victory, the narrowest in a presidential contest in the state's history. In Pennsylvania, his margin of victory was 0.7 percent, the tightest state outcome in a presidential race since William Henry Harrison defeated Martin Van Buren in 1840. In Wisconsin, he won by the same slender margin.

Now comes 2020—and as the polls have predicted, the race is again extremely tight. Biden has won the nationwide popular vote by over four million votes, a larger margin than Clinton, but everything once again turns on the results in our three swing states.

At exactly 11:00 p.m. EST on election day, Fox News projects that Donald Trump has been reelected. But the margin of victory in

our battleground states is even smaller than in 2016. He has carried
Michigan by a scant eight thousand votes; in Wisconsin, the total
falls short of five thousand votes; and in Pennsylvania it is eleven
thousand. As his lead holds through the night, other networks also
declare him the winner. Only MSNBC and CNN, noting that an
unusually large number of absentee and provisional ballots must
still be counted, announce they cannot declare a winner.

In the coming days, as the counts from these ballots begin to
trickle in, CNN's and MSNBC's caution is rewarded. In recent
elections, voters' use of absentee ballots has ticked steadily upward;
in 2016, nearly twenty-five million absentee votes were cast, and the
COVID-19 outbreak promises to dramatically increase the number of absentee voters in 2020.[1] Even without a pandemic to worry
about, Americans, unlike voters in most other modern democracies,
must carve the time to vote out of an ordinary workday. Indeed,
our current election date—the first Tuesday after the first Monday
in November—was adopted in 1845 to accommodate farmers, the
date falling between the completion of the fall harvest and the heavy
snows of winter.

Recent efforts to make election day a holiday have met with stiff
Republican resistance, with Mitch McConnell denouncing such a
plan as a Democratic "power grab."[2] All states, however, allow for
some form of absentee voting. And while absentee ballots have
become ever more popular in recent elections, the technology used
to file them remains distinctly nineteenth-century: Fill out a form,
sign and seal an envelope, affix a stamp, and head to the nearest
mailbox. As an election activist in Pennsylvania put it, "It's just
absurd...to be basically back in the Pony Express era."[3]

Absurd, but maybe not all that terrible, given the enticements
computerized voting offers hackers. Yet relying on the mail service

creates problems of its own. For one thing, states get to decide when an absentee ballot must be submitted. In the case of Pennsylvania, one of our swing states, all absentee ballots must be received by 5:00 p.m. on the Friday *before the election*. Ballots that arrive after that—even those that arrive before the end of election day—simply do not count. American citizens abroad, meanwhile, including members of the military, are also entitled to submit an absentee ballot; in these cases, a different, and typically more accommodating, timetable applies. In Pennsylvania, overseas ballots postmarked by 11:59 p.m. the day before election day will be counted provided they arrive no later than one week *after* election day.

The process of validating an absentee ballot is not simply a matter of checking a postmark, opening an envelope, and feeding a ballot into a high-speed scanner. Counting absentee ballots often requires discretionary judgments on the part of untrained, beleaguered, and partisan local officials. Officials typically must ensure that the voter's signature on the absentee ballot envelope matches one on file. A mismatch is cause for rejection, with no recourse for the voter to affirm that the signature is indeed his. The result is disenfranchisement—without the voter's knowledge.

Provisional ballots, which now account for nearly 2 percent of the total votes cast, pose similar if not greater challenges.[4] The Help America Vote Act, or HAVA—passed, as we've noted, by Congress in the wake of the 2000 election mess—was designed in part to help voters who encounter problems at a voting station.[5] A voter might, for example, show up to vote only to find that their name has been stricken from the electoral rolls, or that the rolls record an incorrect name or address. Alternatively, a voter might have forgotten to bring a photo ID in a jurisdiction that requires one. HAVA permits such persons to submit a provisional ballot.

But before a provisional ballot can be counted, the state must verify that the voter was in fact eligible. This takes both people and time, with time limits statutorily set by each state. In the case of Michigan, local election officials must determine whether a ballot can be counted "within six calendar days after the election." In Pennsylvania, officials have a week, and in Wisconsin, they have until "4:00 pm of the Friday following the election."

While HAVA requires, with a few exceptions, that states make provisional ballots available, it does not mandate how they go about accepting them. In 2016, some 2.5 million provisional ballots were issued, of which only 1.7 million were counted—nearly one out of every three provisional ballots was discarded.[6] And yet the bulk of rejections were the result of mistakes that, depending on where one lives, might or might not count as a cause for disallowing. Some states, for example, count provisional ballots cast in the wrong jurisdiction or precinct, while others toss them.[7] The difference is stark and categorical, and points to a worrisome arbitrariness in how state laws treat such ballots. Indeed, the 30 percent national rejection rate conceals a disturbing disparity—some states count virtually all provisional ballots, while others reject more than half.

Even if all runs smoothly and as planned, states will not be able to fix a final count of their votes until at least a week to ten days after election day. In races in which the outcome is clear, the final tally is largely an errand of bookkeeping. But not in tight races. There, the outcome may very well turn on the results of the absentee and provisional ballots. And the race in 2020 proves very tight indeed.

As Michigan, Wisconsin, and Pennsylvania continue counting their absentee and provisional ballots, a clear pattern begins to emerge. President Trump's lead over Joe Biden is shrinking, and within days, it vanishes altogether. By the time the three states have completed their canvass of votes, the nation faces an astonishing result. *Biden now leads in all three states.* If these leads hold up, he will enjoy an electoral majority and become our next president.

This phenomenon—in which absentee and provisional ballots typically break Democratic—has been dubbed "blue shift" by election law expert Ned Foley.[8] The reasons for the shift are not difficult to divine. The bulk of absentee and provisional ballots are cast in urban areas, where Democratic voters predominate. Indeed, many of the regulations that lead voters to cast provisional ballots, such as the need to supply photo ID, have been designed, as we've seen, not to eliminate fraud, of which there is little, but to make voting more difficult for precisely those groups that might lack standard forms of identification—minorities and the urban poor, groups that vote overwhelmingly Democratic.

The effects of blue shift have been felt in many recent elections, at all levels. The 2018 Arizona senatorial race witnessed a particularly dramatic case. On election day, Martha McSally, the GOP candidate, enjoyed a fifteen-thousand-vote lead over her Democratic rival, Kyrsten Sinema. By the time the state's canvassing had ended, however, McSally found herself defeated by Sinema by some fifty-six thousand votes—a swing of seventy-one thousand.[9] The 2018 senatorial and gubernatorial races in Florida also saw blue shift at work. In the Senate race, Republican Rick Scott's lead over Bill Nelson shrank from over fifty-six thousand on election day to an uncomfortable ten thousand.[10] In the race for governor, Republican Ron DeSantis's election day lead over Democrat Andrew Gillum also fell by nearly forty thousand votes.[11]

In neither Florida race did blue shift overturn the election day outcome. Still, as the lead for the two Republicans began to erode, anxiety spiked in Republican circles, resulting in frantic and troubling attacks on the counting procedure. Leading the way was President Trump, who issued the following demand on Twitter:

> The Florida Election should be called in favor of Rick Scott and Ron DeSantis in that large numbers of ballots showed up from nowhere, and many ballots are missing or forged. An honest vote count is no longer possible—ballots massively infected. Must go with Election Night![12]

Florida senator Marco Rubio and congressman Matt Gaetz, both Republicans, joined the president in suggesting that untoward practices stood behind the threatening gains for Nelson and Gillum. Rubio openly lamented the influx of "Democratic lawyers" descending on the state in order to "change the results of the election."[13]

Former House Speaker Paul Ryan joined in casting doubts on blue shift. Commenting on a handful of California congressional races, he complained, "We had lots of wins that night and three weeks later we lost basically every contested CA race."[14] The losses, Ryan insisted, were "bizarre."

And in 2016, Trump himself felt the effects of blue shift. In Pennsylvania, his lead over Clinton shrank from sixty-eight thousand on election day to forty-four thousand by the time the state officially certified its results.

That drop proved to be of little consequence. Not so in our 2020 scenario. As the tallies finish, a shift of twenty-five thousand votes has completely wiped out Trump's election day lead of eleven thousand—and has him losing Pennsylvania by some fourteen thousand votes. Similar shifts in Wisconsin and Michigan leave him trailing in these states too. Trump faces defeat.

None of this catches the president unprepared. Since being declared victorious by Fox on election day, he has been tweeting tirelessly, reprising the same demands and claims he made in 2018 when Scott and DeSantis saw their leads slip in Florida.

> In interest of FAIRNESS, ELECTION must be CALLED NOW! We must STOP the CORRUPT Democrats in PA, MI & WI from STEALING our VICTORY with THOUSANDS of FAKE VOTES!!!
>
> * * *
>
> DEMS will never STOP trying to STEAL an election they can't win HONESTLY! MUST go with ELECTION DAY COUNT!!
>
> * * *
>
> Stories of DISGUSTING FRAUD pouring in from MICHIGAN!! Dems can't win honestly, so they CHEAT!! Courts must STOP this FRAUD!!

While Trump's claims of fraud lack merit, they find support among his various megaphones in Congress and the media and gain traction with his supporters, who, like millions of other Americans, cannot fathom how tens of thousands of votes can seemingly materialize after election day. Back in 2000, as recounts saw George W. Bush's lead in Florida shrink, Fox's Sean Hannity repeatedly accused Al Gore of trying to "steal the election."[15] Members of an extremist paramilitary group, the "Minutemen," converged in Florida, armed and prepared to fight. As one Minuteman put it, "I'm out here because if Gore is allowed to prevail, we will no longer live in a country with the rule of law."[16] Now multiple paramilitary groups announce they will fight a Biden presidency.

Further complicating matters, the *New York Times* and the *Wall Street Journal* report that in a handful of districts in Wisconsin, Michigan, and Pennsylvania, election officials have accidentally mixed together a small number of valid and invalid provisional ballots, muddying the recount. Something quite similar happened in Broward County—yes, *that* Broward County—in 2018, during the Scott and DeSantis canvassing. Only now, Trump's tweets and the echo chamber of right-wing social media magnify these small acts of incompetence and confusion into a grand, organized conspiracy to overturn the results of election day.

Trump's lawyers, aided by the Justice Department, file suit to strike the provisional ballots in the three battleground states.[17] A federal judge—a Trump appointee—concludes that a fair and accurate result cannot include the provisional ballots, and instructs state election officials in all three states to disqualify them.

Biden appeals, and though he ultimately wins, the appellate process chews up time, and as a result, the three states all fail to complete their canvass until December 19—eleven days after the "safe harbor" deadline has passed and five days after electors have met across the nation. Recall, the safe harbor date was fixed by the Electoral Count Act of 1887 as a way of encouraging states to settle their electoral disputes before they reach Congress.

In *Bush v. Gore*, the Supreme Court notoriously used the fact that a recount would inevitably carry Florida past the safe harbor deadline to call a halt to the Gore recount.[18] Congress, however, has only once come close to activating ECA's safe harbor provision. That came in the wake of the 1960 election between Nixon and Kennedy. On election day, Nixon appeared to carry Hawaii by a scant 141 votes and the outgoing governor certified Nixon's electors and sent the result to Congress. In the meantime, Democrats petitioned for a recount, which wasn't completed until late December. On December 30, a state court declared Kennedy the winner in Hawaii by 115 votes, and the newly elected governor certified *that* result and sent it on to Congress. Further complicating matters, Kennedy's electors sent their own certificate too, so on January 6, 1961, Congress found itself confronted with three separate certificates from the same state—one certified by the departing governor, and filed by the safe harbor deadline; a second, certified by the incoming governor, filed after the deadline; and a third, filed directly by electors, also after the deadline.

Had Congress activated ECA procedure, it would presumably have accepted the first certificate; after all, this was the one certified by the chief executive and enjoying safe harbor. But this never happened. Nixon, who was still vice president and so presided over the electoral count in the joint session, chose to accept the second certificate. He did so, Nixon announced, "in order not to delay the further count of the electoral vote" but *without the intent of establishing a precedent*" (italics added). No objections were raised; Hawaii went to Kennedy, and nothing turned on the outcome.[19]

In 2020, things are very different. Wisconsin, Pennsylvania, and Michigan share a common political profile: In each, the state legislature is controlled by Republicans, while the governor is a Democrat. Because of delays in the final canvassing of votes, the Republican legislatures in all three states vote on December 8 to recognize the election day outcome. Six days later, on December 14, Trump's electors meet in Madison, Harrisburg, and Lansing to cast their votes for Trump. The respective legislatures certify these results and send them to Congress.

The Democratic governors—Tony Evers of Wisconsin, Tom Wolf of Pennsylvania, and Gretchen Whitmer of Michigan—express outrage that the legislatures have acted before the full vote counts could be completed. On December 19, Wisconsin, Pennsylvania, and Michigan finally finish their canvasses, and the results underscore the reality and power of blue shift. Biden has won the popular vote in all three states. His electors meet in all three state capitals, casting their votes for the former vice president, and the three Democratic governors certify and forward these results to Congress.

Come January 6, when the joint session of Congress convenes, things take a quick and ugly turn. As in the 1876 election, three states have each submitted two certificates. And each pair of certificates shares the identical profile: The first, certified by the legislature, complies with the safe harbor provision; the second, certified by the governor, does not. Challenges are raised against both, and the two chambers separate to fruitlessly debate the matter. Republicans insist that by the terms of the Electoral Count Act of 1887, the safe harbor certificate carries the day. Democrats respond that the ECA privileges the certificate endorsed by the state's chief executive. Not true, answer Republicans—the ECA gives the nod to the governor's certificate only in cases in which both certificates fail the safe harbor deadline. Democrats counter that by certifying a result before the completion of the states' canvasses, the states' legislatures violated basic norms of democracy. Republicans argue that the canvasses were muddied by corruption, and moreover that it's not Congress's role to second-guess the states. Democrats insist there was no corruption, just incompetence that had no effect on the outcome.

At last debate ends, the chambers vote, and the results follow their foreordained course. The Republican-controlled Senate rejects the governors' certificates and accepts the legislatures'; the Democrat-controlled House votes in precisely the opposite fashion.

Meltdown. The nation finds itself in much the same situation that we encountered in our first two catastrophe scenarios. Both parties appeal to the Supreme Court, but as we've seen, it's far from clear that the high court would agree to intervene in the matter—or, if it did, that Trump and Republican lawmakers would recognize its jurisdiction or abide by an unfavorable holding. Any decision one way or the other seems guaranteed to result in a complete revolt of the losing party's lawmakers, both in the capital and nationwide.

And so again we find ourselves at noon on January 20 without an elected president—or, rather, with two persons claiming to have won the election, and a third, Nancy Pelosi, announcing that she has resigned her speakership so she can perform her legally authorized role as acting president until the impasse can be resolved. Trump warns of "civil war," and in protests across the country, Trump and Biden supporters clash violently. Trump tweets, "PATRIOTIC AMERICANS are understandably ANGRY!! Things will get WORSE before they get better. Maybe MUCH WORSE!!"

CHAPTER 16

Can the Crisis Be Contained?

How does our story end? With the forty-fifth president of the United States barricaded in the Oval Office, surrounded by a phalanx of rogue Secret Service agents, hysterically tweeting that he is the nation's true and only president?

Such a dire scenario is by no means impossible, but we need not entertain a Hollywood finale in order to appreciate the damage that could result from the 2020 election going sideways. Clearly, things could go wrong in ways different from what we have imagined in our three crisis scenarios. As we noted at the outset, it is certainly possible that Trump will win reelection. His victory would represent yet another singular failure of the Electoral College, for while Trump could secure 270 Electoral College votes, it is unlikely that he could ever capture the popular vote; and for the third time this century, the popular-vote loser would become the president. Alternately, in a close electoral defeat, Trump could simply reject the results in whichever swing states cost him the election. We know that Trump is not above claiming fraud where there is none and denying fraud that is real—particularly if orchestrated by Russia.

We can also confidently predict that even should Trump voluntarily leave the White House, he will do so without ever conceding defeat. Trump will never recognize the legitimacy of any contest in which he loses. In 2016, when Senator Ted Cruz defeated him in the Iowa caucus, Trump briefly accepted his loss. By the next day, however, he had assumed a more characteristic stance, tweeting that "Ted Cruz didn't win Iowa, he stole it." That tweet was followed with a second: "Based on the fraud committed by Senator Ted Cruz during the Iowa Caucus, either a new election should take place or Cruz [*sic*] results nullified."[1]

The best we can expect from President Donald Trump after an electoral defeat is self-pitying, peevish submission. As president, he has proven extraordinarily successful in fostering and strengthening a bond of shared grievance with his base. In leaving office, he will strive to keep this connection alive. To do so, he must make sure that he is seen not as a loser, but as a victim of the same nefarious Deep State forces that allegedly have been aligned against him since the moment he took office. He will insist that he has been forced from office precisely because he kept faith with his base. In defeat, his brand will remain irresistible to his supporters.

Even in this best-case scenario, Trump will leave the new administration—and the nation—in a perilously weakened state. It is the responsibility of an outgoing administration to prepare the incoming president so that power transfers smoothly—President Obama, for instance, praised George W. Bush and the members of his administration for their professionalism and helpfulness in preparing the new administration to assume the reins of power. But in a display of incompetence and spite, Trump and his team will leave the White House in an utterly chaotic state, purposively complicating Biden's task of governance.

It is not hard to play out this dismal scenario. Trump will surely cap his refusal to facilitate the transition of power by boycotting Biden's inauguration.[2] Having refused to concede, and continuing to insist that rampant domestic fraud and foreign interference cost him victory, he tweets that he will not attend "the SHAM inauguration of a SHAM president!!" Grudgingly he announces that he will leave the White House—but not on January 20. Using a manufactured domestic or international crisis as an excuse to linger in the White House, he insists that while Biden was planning his inaugural ball, he was saving the nation from threats and so has been unable to plan a timely departure.

Consider the consequences of Trump's staying in the White House for even one extra day. Andrew Johnson granted Mary Todd Lincoln extra time to leave the White House, a courtesy that Lyndon Johnson also extended to Jackie Kennedy. But President Biden finds himself in a completely different situation. Ordering Trump's immediate removal would inflame his base and make the new president look insecure and vindictive, while tolerating his tarrying would signal confusion and weakness, especially should Trump decide to turn one day into two, and two into three. Assuming Trump ultimately does leave—say, a week after Biden's inauguration—he would have succeeded in transforming the meaning of the act of departure. It would no longer be a constitutionally and legally compulsory move mandated by electoral defeat; it would now look like a matter of choice. Trump has *chosen* to leave office—the implication being that he might have chosen otherwise. In leaving, he confirms rather than relinquishes his power.

And by leaving without conceding, Trump guarantees that millions of Americans will view the new administration as illegitimate. Keeping himself in the spotlight, he will be able to exercise destabilizing power from the instant he leaves the White House. The Trump International Hotel, housed in the Old Post Office just a half mile from the White House, could supply him with a new base of operations from which he and Sean Hannity launch their planned cable news network. With millions of die-hard supporters firmly believing that their president has been toppled by the machinations of a malignant Deep State, Trump could remain a force of chaos for years to come. Indeed, having lost in 2020, he could run again in 2024.

Alas, we can imagine much worse. During the Watergate scandal, then–secretary of defense James Schlesinger became so alarmed that President Nixon or one of his aides "might get in touch with some military units" in order to block the "constitutional process" that he made sure no unauthorized orders were given to military units by the White House.[3] Whether Schlesinger was responding to a real threat can be debated; in Trump's case, the danger that the president could trigger a military crisis to nullify an election is hardly far-fetched. Trump's ill-advised decision, in January 2020, to order the killing of Major General Qassim Suleimani, Iran's second most important official, seems to have been motivated, at least in part, by the desire to deflect attention away from his impeachment.

How, then, might Trump behave in the days following a contested electoral defeat? We need not imagine him consciously choosing to endanger tens of thousands of Americans in order to protect himself politically. The point is that this most impulsive of presidents, who has gutted the nation's national security apparatus and responds to provocations without weighing the larger consequences of his actions, sees no difference between the nation's strategic interests and his own political fortunes. He could catapult us into a catastrophic war in an act of reckless narcissism. Or he could, as Schlesinger feared, order the military into Washington to keep him installed in power.

Would the military defy Trump? The 1962 thriller *Seven Days in May* imagined an attempted coup against a duly elected president orchestrated by renegade members of the armed forces—a scenario then-president Kennedy did not consider far-fetched. Our nightmare imagines the obverse: a renegade president, acting in defiance of the Constitution, propelling us into war and a state of domestic upheaval. How would the Pentagon react? To ask the question is to imagine a world gone horribly awry. No member of the nation's military leadership wants to be thrust into the position of deciding whether to defy or remove the commander in chief. An America in which the military is thrust into that position is an America we don't know and don't want to know. And yet Trump might leave us no other choice.

So things can go very wrong in 2020 in ways different from what we have imagined. But our three scenarios remind us how a series of events could trigger a meltdown in our electoral process. None of the scenarios are probable; on the other hand, none of them are all that *improbable*. Electors have acted "faithlessly" in the past; our system is clearly vulnerable to hacking and interference; and states have submitted conflicting electoral certificates. The system seriously misfired in 1800, 1876, and 2000; came close to misfiring in 1880, 1884, and 1888;[4] and suffered clear, though ultimately manageable, malfunctions in 1960 (contradictory certificates from Hawaii), 1968 (faithless elector challenged in Congress), and 2016 (faithless electors and the election of the popular-vote loser).

In none of these cases did the system completely melt down—but not thanks to any fail-safe backup plans. To the contrary, we have seen that far from supplying a blueprint for de-escalation, our Constitution and laws have gross gaps and troubling opacities that would nudge a crisis forward. In 1876 and 2000, we were spared catastrophe thanks to the character of the losing candidates. In 1877, violence was averted because Samuel Tilden placed national reconciliation above his own personal interest. In 2000, when chaos threatened, Al Gore made the same choice. Does anyone believe Trump would act similarly?

CHAPTER 17

Republicans Reject Democracy

Our crisis scenarios share a common feature. They all assume that congressional Republicans will continue to support Trump in his attempt to hold on to office following a narrow and bitterly contested electoral defeat. Trump's ability to engage in constitutional defiance depends directly on this support. Should congressional Republicans choose to recognize Biden's victory—should they, for example, accept Detroit's recount in our second scenario, or acknowledge the reality of blue shift in our third—Trump's ability to hold on to power would be seriously checked.

The key figure here is Senate majority leader Mitch McConnell. If McConnell signals that he will not abide by Trump's defiance, then Trump would have very little choice but to submit to defeat, even if he never actually conceded. Such a scenario presupposes McConnell's continued ability to control a sizable number of his Republican senatorial colleagues. Of course, even then Trump could still make things difficult for "disloyal" Republicans. Appealing directly to his base by Twitter, he could accuse McConnell of treasonous backstabbing and cowardly betrayal, charges that would no doubt find sympathy and support from Trump's most dependable media megaphones.

But anyone hopeful that Mitch McConnell and his Republican colleagues might defy Trump has not been paying attention to American politics over the last several years. We need not list all the former stalwart opponents of Trump, such as Senator Lindsey Graham, who have turned into apologists—or the specious excuses that congressional Republicans trotted out to justify refusing to call former national security advisor John Bolton to testify in Trump's impeachment trial.

And yet it would be wrong to conclude that Republicans have fallen in line behind Trump simply because they believe that doing so is necessary to remain politically viable. This no doubt explains the behavior of some congressional Republicans; but the sad reality is that in the past decade, the politics of negation has become a central feature of Republican political behavior. The recent Republican credo can be summarized thus: *Elections—and governmental processes generally—are to be respected only when we prevail.*

Recall Mitch McConnell's stunning refusal to grant a hearing to Merrick Garland, President Obama's nominee to fill the Supreme Court vacancy left by Justice Antonin Scalia's death. The Constitution empowers the president to nominate justices and tasks the Senate with confirming or rejecting them. In a 150-year span—from 1866 to 2016—the Senate never once prevented a president from ultimately filling a Supreme Court vacancy.[1] McConnell's refusal to consider Obama's choice was more than a break with precedent; it was an act of electoral nullification. During the 2016 election, Ted Cruz, among other GOP senators, went one step further, vowing in advance to block any nomination that Clinton, had she won, might make to the Supreme Court.[2]

Consider also Senate Republicans' use of the filibuster during Obama's presidency. From the time that cloture rules were introduced into the Senate in 1917 until the end of Reagan's presidency, the filibuster was deployed 385 times. During Obama's presidency, Senate Republicans launched over 500 filibusters, many of them to directly block Obama's appointments to the federal bench.[3] In Republican hands the filibuster ceased to be a tool of checks and balances and became a tool of obstruction—or, more precisely, nullification.

To this we can add McConnell's refusal to sign on to a bipartisan statement condemning Russian interference in the 2016 election.[4] Well before the election, the Obama administration shared with leaders of Congress intelligence documenting Russian interference. President Obama rightly believed that a public condemnation of Russia required a show of bipartisanship. But while then–House leader Paul Ryan agreed to sign on to the statement, McConnell refused. Instead, he threatened to accuse Obama of trying to influence the outcome for Clinton should the administration issue a statement of condemnation.[5] And so an effort to craft a bipartisan statement designed to protect the integrity of a presidential election came to naught.[6]

The GOP's electoral defiance has operated no less aggressively on the state level. In the 2016 gubernatorial race in North Carolina, Democrat Roy Cooper edged out Republican incumbent Pat McCrory. McCrory at first refused to concede, blaming his loss on baseless allegations of voter fraud; then, once it became clear that Cooper would become the next governor, the Republican-controlled state legislature promptly rewrote the chief executive's job description, stripping Cooper of powers that previous governors had enjoyed.[7]

Wisconsin, one of our battleground states, witnessed a similar spectacle. In 2018, Democrat Tony Evers won the gubernatorial race, unseating Republican incumbent Scott Walker. Here, too, the Republican-controlled legislature promptly rewrote the law to strip the governor of essential powers. And in 2018, another battleground state, Michigan, saw Democrat Gretchen Whitmer trounce her Republican rival in capturing the governorship. Again, Republican state lawmakers raced to strip the state's chief executive of crucial powers, though those efforts ultimately failed.[8]

Republican state legislators in Oregon went even further. Determined to deny the majority Democrats a quorum necessary to pass legislation responsive to climate change, in June 2019, Republican lawmakers simply refused to show up for work, with some going into hiding. When Governor Kate Brown directed the state police to bring the AWOL lawmakers back to the Capitol, a Republican state senator warned that the officers had better "come heavily armed" because "I'm not going to be a political prisoner in the state of Oregon." Right-wing paramilitary groups rushed to the defense of the Republican lawmakers, threatening civil war and causing the state police to cancel a session of the state senate because of a "credible threat" from a militia group.[9]

Trump, then, is hardly alone in waging a politics of democratic nullification. As one expert has observed, "Republicans are now... the best example for a concerted attack on democratic norms perpetrated by a nominally establishment party."[10]

All the same, it would be wrong to conclude, as many have, that "Trump is as much a symptom of the current crisis as he is a cause."[11] Trump explodes such simple binaries. Think of the wildfires in California. Local fires break out, but these are small and containable. Then along comes a ferocious wind that blows hot, hard, and long. Blazes that might have been contained now join up and rage out of control, the damage untold.

CHAPTER 18

The Only Check

If congressional Republicans are far more likely to aid and abet Trump's electoral defiance than to restrain it, where might restraint come from? Abolishing the Electoral College and replacing it with a system of direct election with an instant runoff would certainly be a healthy change. All at once, three noxious outcomes would be averted: The popular-vote loser could no longer capture the White House; in a multicandidate race, the plurality winner could no longer become president despite lacking majority support; and finally, a national election would no longer turn on what happens in a handful of closely divided swing states.

Abolishing the Electoral College, however, is liable to remain impossible, as we have seen. But other, more modest reforms are within our reach. The Wolf Blitzers, John Kings, and Anderson Coopers of the world can be tutored to remind their viewers on election day that the results they announce are tentative, pending the count of absentee and provisional ballots. They can instruct their viewers to expect a blue shift as these votes are counted, and that this shift may very well change the outcome. That the likes of Sean Hannity, Laura Ingraham, and Mark Levin will act in reckless disregard of these facts does not diminish the public service that can be performed by reminding Americans of these realities.

Establishing national standards for election technology and cybersecurity would also be welcome. As we have seen, the nation has eight thousand distinct voting districts, with ballots and machines varying from district to district. States have their own laws and standards for verifying absentee and provisional ballots. Such complexity creates arbitrariness and invites abuse. Making our system less vulnerable to accidents and manipulation will require money—money that must come from Congress in the form of an ongoing commitment. Safeguarding our electoral system should be such an obvious priority that it beggars belief that it, too, has been made into a bitterly partisan issue by Republican lawmakers.

We should create impartial, nonpartisan electoral commissions responsible for monitoring elections and tabulating results. As one expert has observed, the United States is "alone among the world's democracies" in allowing "partisan officials...to be in charge of election administrations."[1] Recall that in Florida in 2000, the secretary of state responsible for administering the election, Katherine Harris, was the co-chair of the Bush-Cheney campaign in Florida, while the state's attorney general, Bob Butterworth, was the chair of Gore's Florida campaign. Leaving the count in the hands of partisans is obviously unwise, if for no other reason than it erodes confidence in the trustworthiness of outcomes—an essential element of electoral legitimacy.

And should a genuine crisis materialize, we need a dedicated, impartial, and well-prepared body capable of adjudicating a resolution. Luck and the very strength of American democratic norms have permitted us to get away with an obviously defective method of troubleshooting electoral disputes. With those norms under assault, we can no longer afford to entrust our democracy to such faulty processes.

Several Latin American countries have created independent electoral tribunals, special branches of the judiciary with their jurisdiction specifically limited to electoral matters.[2] In the 1990s, Mexico created a supreme electoral tribunal, which has aided the country's move away from one-party rule and helped Mexico avoid a political meltdown in 2006, when the presidential election produced a Bush-versus-Gore-like result.[3] We would well benefit from the creation of such a body. As proposed by Ned Foley, this electoral count tribunal would be empowered to adjudicate disputed cases, and its decisions would be binding unless overturned by both houses of Congress.[4]

Removing Congress altogether from its role in counting and accepting electoral votes would of course require a constitutional amendment and so poses all the problems associated with that arduous process. Even an electoral tribunal created by statute would raise questions about how to guarantee its independence and neutrality. And even assuming that a suitable design *could* be agreed upon, change will certainly not come by November 2020. Alas, it is precisely the kind of fiasco we might confront in our next election that could create the political will necessary for reform.

A Trump win in 2020 would be a catastrophe for the country. A man manifestly unfit for higher office, an opportunistic and habitual liar with a contempt for constitutional governance and the rule of law, would have four additional years to attack the free press, deform our foreign policy, weaken our alliances, erode our regulatory structures, undermine efforts to address climate change, attack the neutral administration of justice, and disfigure the composition of the federal judiciary. If it happens, what in 2016 looked like a disturbing aberration begins to assume the lineaments of a permanent shift. The carnage becomes real and lasting.

And then there is the specter that has animated our discussion—that an uncertain or close result in 2020 will enable Trump to catapult the nation into a crisis of peaceful succession. This would represent a greater disaster for America than an outright victory by Trump. In the end, the most reliable check on this outcome lies not in our laws or Constitution but in the hands of the American people. Should voters give Democrats majorities in both the House and the Senate, Trump will find himself limited in his power to mount a catastrophic challenge to a contested result. He could cause chaos, but not a meltdown.

Likewise, should Trump suffer a decisive defeat on November 3, 2020, his claims of hoax and fraud will find traction only with his most fervent supporters.

And yet it's hard to imagine Trump suffering such an emphatic electoral loss. Far more likely is his victory, perhaps aided by voter suppression, disinformation, and foreign meddling—or the kind of uncertain result that will leave the nation vulnerable to Trump's politics of constitutional brinkmanship. In either case, American democracy will find itself in a state of peril last seen during the horrors of the Civil War.

ACKNOWLEDGMENTS

This book could not have been written without the support of a fellowship from the Carnegie Foundation and the generosity of Amherst College; at Amherst, I'm particularly grateful to President Biddy Martin and the Dean of Faculty, Catherine Epstein.

Will He Go? developed out of opinion pieces that I've been writing for the *Guardian* since Trump took office. I'd like to thank Amana Fontanella-Khan, my editor at the *Guardian*, for her smart and steady editorial hand. Still, it was my terrific agent, Daniel Greenberg, and the peerless editor of Twelve, Sean Desmond, who saw a book in these pieces.

As I began work on *Will He Go?*, I received extremely helpful guidance from Ian Bassin and Chris Vaeth of Protect Democracy. I'm also grateful to the folks at the Bipartisan Policy Center for inviting me to their election workshop. Norbert Frei at the University of Jena gave me an early opportunity to share some of my thoughts (in German!) about the Trump presidency.

When it came to framing my research and argument, I received valuable suggestions from Steve Berman, Alex George, Viveca Greene, John Kleiner, Betsy Kolbert, Laura Moser, Nishi Shah, and my wife, Nancy Pick. I also greatly benefited from my interviews with several persons who have chosen to remain unnamed.

I'm grateful to Owen Fiss, Ned Foley, Rick Hasen, Cullen

Murphy, Paul Smith, and Larry Tribe for their extremely helpful comments on the manuscript. Ned Foley and Larry Tribe, in particular, demonstrated exceptional generosity and insight in helping me refine things, while Owen Fiss, mentor and friend, provided crucial support and wisdom. And Rand Cooper did his magic.

I'd also like to thank my colleagues in the Department of Law, Jurisprudence & Social Thought at Amherst: Michaela Brangan, David Delaney, Mona Oraby, Austin Sarat, Adam Sitze, and Martha Umphrey. I also benefited from the help of our departmental coordinator, Megan Estes, and my two student assistants, Jacob Schulz and Charles Sutherby.

At Twelve, thanks go to the whole outstanding team—Sean, Rachel Kambury, Bob Castillo, Paul Samuelson, Jarrod Taylor, Brian McLendon, Joseph Benincase, and Daniel Modlin. Finally, I extend something well beyond gratitude to my wife, Nancy Pick, and our sons, Jacob and Milo. May we all know a healthy democratic future.

ENDNOTES

Chapter 2: *Trump Rejects Defeat*

1. Quoted in Nicholas Kristof, "We Will Survive. Probably," *New York Times,* March 6, 2019, www.nytimes.com/2019/03/06/opinion/michael-cohen-trump.html.

2. Glenn Thrush, "Pelosi Warns Democrats: Stay in the Center or Trump May Contest Election Results," *New York Times*, May 4, 2019, www.nytimes.com/2019/05/04/us/politics/nancy-pelosi.html.

3. Trip Gabriel, "Donald Trump's Call to Monitor Polls Raises Fears of Intimidation," *New York Times*, October 18, 2016, www.nytimes.com/2016/10/19/us/politics/donald-trump-voting-election-rigging.html.

4. Steven Levitsky and Daniel Ziblatt, *How Democracies Die* (New York: Crown, 2018), 61.

5. "Transcript of the Third Debate," *New York Times*, October 20, 2016, www.nytimes.com/2016/10/20/us/politics/third-debate-transcript.html.

6. True, our history has not been free of candidates refusing to acknowledge defeat. In 2018, Democratic candidate Stacey Abrams refused to concede in the Georgia gubernatorial race, alleging election fraud. Yet in Abrams's case, the claims of voter suppression had merit; Abrams's opponent in the race, Brian Kemp, was at the time serving as Georgia's chief elections officer, and one expert described his electoral shenanigans as "the most banana republic moment in the United States that I could recall." See Richard L. Hasen, *Election Meltdown: Dirty Tricks, Distrust, and the Threat to American Democracy* (New Haven, CT: Yale University Press, 2020), 66.

    Still, Abrams's claim that she'd "won" the race remains troubling, despite her attempts in an interview in the *New York Times Magazine* to distinguish her stance from Trump's and to insist, "My larger point is…I won because we transformed the electorate, we turned out people who had never voted, we outmatched every Democrat in Georgia history." "Why Stacey Abrams Is Still Saying She Won," *New York Times Magazine*, April 28, 2019, www.nytimes.com/interactive/2019/04/28/magazine/stacey-abrams-election-georgia.html.

7. Levitsky and Ziblatt, *How Democracies Die*, 61.

8. Anthony Zurcher, "Trump 'Might Not Accept Election Result,'" BBC News, October 20, 2016, www.bbc.com/news/election-us-2016-37706499.
9. Mattathias Schwartz, "Obama Had a Secret Plan in Case Trump Rejected 2016 Election Results," Daily Intelligencer, *New York* magazine, October 10, 2018, nymag.com/intelligencer/2018/10/obama-had-a-secret-plan-in-case-trump-rejected-2016-results.html.

Chapter 3: *Trump Rejects Victory*

1. Glenn Thrush, "Trump's Voter Fraud Example? A Troubled Tale with Bernhard Langer," *New York Times*, January 25, 2017, www.nytimes.com/2017/01/25/us/politics/trump-bernhard-langer-voting-fraud.html.
2. Zack Beauchamp, "Trump's Attack on the Florida Recounts Is an Attack on American Democracy," *Vox*, November 12, 2018, www.vox.com/policy-and-politics/2018/11/12/18088048/trump-florida-recount-senate-rick-scott-democracy.

Chapter 4: *Elections the Authoritarian Way*

1. Samuel Issacharoff, *Fragile Democracies: Contested Power in the Era of Constitutional Courts* (Cambridge Studies in Election Law and Democracy) (New York: Cambridge University Press, 2015), 3.
2. "Play Fair: How to Prevent a Corrupt President from Tipping the Playing Field in His Own Election," white paper, Protect Democracy, July 2019, https://protectdemocracy.org/preventing-and-deterring-election-manipulation/election-manipulation-white-paper/, 6.
3. "Play Fair," 6.
4. Benjamin Carter Hett, *The Death of Democracy: Hitler's Rise to Power and the Downfall of the Weimar Republic* (New York: Henry Holt, 2018), 83–84. The closest thing to an emergency provision in our Constitution is the suspension clause in Article I, Section 9, which authorizes Congress to suspend habeas corpus in cases of invasion or rebellion.
5. Helene Cooper, "Jim Mattis, Defense Secretary, Resigns in Rebuke of Trump's Worldview," *New York Times*, December 20, 2018, www.nytimes.com/2018/12/20/us/politics/jim-mattis-defense-secretary-trump.html.
6. "Read Fiona Hill's Opening Statement," *New York Times*, November 21, 2019, www.nytimes.com/interactive/2019/11/21/us/politics/fiona-hill-opening-statement-ukraine.html.
7. Colby Itkowitz and Reis Thebault, "'Almost a Spy': Transcript and Video of Trump's Remarks at Private U.N. Event about Whistleblower," *Washington Post*, September 27, 2019, www.washingtonpost.com/politics/almost-a-spy-transcript-of-trumps-remarks-at-private-un-event-about-whistleblower/2019/09/26/f85477fe-e0bb-11e9-b199-f638bf2c340f_story.html.
8. Donald J. Trump, tweet, November 5, 2018, https://twitter.com/realdonaldtrump/status/1059470847751131138?lang=en.

Chapter 5: *The Peculiar Beauty of Conceding Defeat*

1. "Text of Gore's Concession Speech," *New York Times*, December 13, 2000, www.nytimes.com/2000/12/13/politics/text-of-goreacutes-concession-speech .html.
2. Edward Foley, *Ballot Battles: The History of Disputed Elections in the United States* (New York: Oxford University Press, 2016), 302.

Chapter 6: *So Much for Our Norms*

1. The other two being Andrew Johnson and Bill Clinton. Like Trump, neither Johnson nor Clinton were "convicted" by the Senate. Recall that President Nixon resigned rather than face his inevitable impeachment and removal from office. In 1842, the House voted down a resolution to impeach President John Tyler.
2. Congress could in principle extend the statutory time limit, and prosecutors could also persuasively argue that the statutory period should not begin to run until the immunity from indictment is lifted; otherwise a president could commit crimes with impunity and, perhaps worse still, be perversely incentivized to stay in office for no better reason than to run out the clock on prosecutors. And yet in *Stogner v. California*, 539 U.S. 607 (2003), the Supreme Court struck down a state's retroactive extension of a statute of limitations as a violation of the Constitution's bar against *ex post facto* law. So the system of perverse incentives may very well be in place.
3. Robert Reich, "If Trump Loses, We Know What to Expect: Anger, Fear and Disruption," *Guardian*, March 3, 2019, www.theguardian.com/commentisfree/2019 /mar/03/donald-trump-2020-defeat-michael-cohen.
4. Katie Rogers, "White House Hosts Conservative Internet Activists at a 'Social Media Summit,'" *New York Times*, July 11, 2019, www.nytimes.com/2019/07/11 /us/politics/white-house-social-media-summit.html.
5. Derek Thompson, "Donald J. Trump's Television Future," *Atlantic*, October 18, 2016, www.theatlantic.com/business/archive/2016/10/donald-j-trumps-television -future/504500/.

Chapter 7: *Lies, Damn Lies, and Meta-lies*

1. Hannah Arendt, "Truth and Politics," in *Between Past and Future: Eight Exercises in Political Thought*, enlarged ed. (New York: Viking, 1968), 227.
2. "President Trump made 16,241 false or misleading claims in his first three years," *Washington Post*, updated January 20, 2020, www.washingtonpost.com /graphics/politics/trump-claims-database/.
3. Charles M. Blow, "Lie, Exploit and Destroy," *New York Times*, February 8, 2018, www.nytimes.com/2018/02/08/opinion/trump-lie-mueller-investigation.html.
4. Katie Rogers, "Fact-Checking Trump's Claim He 'Spent a Lot of Time' with 9/11 Responders," *New York Times*, July 29, 2019, www.nytimes.com/2019/07/29 /us/politics/trump-9-11-fact-check.html.

5. Salvador Rizzo, "Trump Falsely Claims He Tried to Stop 'Send Her Back!' Chants About Rep. Ilhan Omar," *Washington Post*, July 18, 2019, www.washingtonpost .com/politics/2019/07/18/trump-falsely-claims-he-tried-stop-send-her-back -chants-about-rep-ilhan-omar/.

6. Donald J. Trump, tweet, September 2, 2019, https://twitter.com/realDonaldTrump /status/1168499355248205826?ref_src=twsrc%5Etfw%7Ctwcamp%5Etweetem bed%7Ctwterm%5E1168517178636800000&ref_url=https%3A%2F%2Fwww .cnn.com%2F2019%2F09%2F02%2Fmedia%2Ftrump-press-attacks -media%2Findex.html.

7. "In His Own Words: The President's Attacks on the Courts," Brennan Center for Justice, June 5, 2017, www.brennancenter.org/our-work/analysis-opinion/his -own-words-presidents-attacks-courts.

Chapter 8: *The Sweet Air of Legitimacy*

1. Charles L. Black, *The People and the Court: Judicial Review in a Democracy* (New York: Macmillan, 1960), 53.

2. Alexander M. Bickel, *The Least Dangerous Branch: The Supreme Court at the Bar of Politics* (Indianapolis: Bobbs-Merrill, 1962), 30.

3. Martin Tolchin, "How Johnson Won Election He'd Lost," *New York Times*, February 11, 1990, www.nytimes.com/1990/02/11/us/how-johnson-won-election -he-d-lost.html.

4. Amy Gardner, "N.C. Election Officials: Harris Operative Collected and Falsified Ballots, Then Tried to Obstruct State Investigation," *Washington Post*, February 18, 2019, www.washingtonpost.com/politics/nc-election-officials -harris-operative-collected-and-falsified-ballots-then-tried-to-obstruct-state -investigation/2019/02/18/6501347a-339a-11e9-854a-7a14d7fec96a_story.html.

5. Alan Blinder, "New Election Ordered in North Carolina Race at Center of Fraud Inquiry," *New York Times*, February 21, 2019, www.nytimes.com/2019/02/21 /us/mark-harris-nc-voter-fraud.html.

6. Susan Page and Deborah Barfield Berry, "Poll: Half of Americans Say Trump Is Victim of a 'Witch Hunt' as Trust in Mueller Erodes," *USA Today*, March 18, 2019, www.usatoday.com/story/news/politics/2019/03/18/trust-mueller-investigation -falls-half-americans-say-trump-victim-witch-hunt/3194049002/.

7. "Republicans Far More Likely than Democrats to Say Fact-Checkers Tend to Favor One Side," *Pew Research Center* (blog), accessed December 15, 2019, www.pewresearch.org/fact-tank/2019/06/27/republicans-far-more-likely-than -democrats-to-say-fact-checkers-tend-to-favor-one-side/.

8. "The State of Free Speech and Tolerance in America," Cato Institute, October 31, 2017, www.cato.org/survey-reports/state-free-speech-tolerance-america.

9. "Americans' Views on the Media: Ipsos Poll on Sentiment Towards American Media," August 7, 2018, www.ipsos.com/sites/default/files/ct/news/documents /2018-08/media_trust_topline_080618_0.pdf.

10. Sam Corbett-Davies, Tobias Konitzer, and David Rothschild, "Poll: 60% of

Republicans Believe Illegal Immigrants Vote; 43% Believe People Vote Using Dead People's Names," *Washington Post*, October 24, 2016, www.washington post.com/news/monkey-cage/wp/2016/10/24/poll-60-of-republicans-believe -illegal-immigrants-vote-43-believe-people-vote-using-dead-peoples-names/.

11. "Many Republicans Doubt Clinton Won Popular Vote," *Morning Consult*, July 26, 2017, www.morningconsult.com/2017/07/26/many-republicans-think-trump -won-2016-popular-vote-didnt/.

12. Levitsky and Ziblatt, *How Democracies Die*, 197.

13. Issacharoff, *Fragile Democracies*, 26.

Chapter 9: *Bootstrapping Meta-lies into Institutional Realities*

1. Hasen, *Election Meltdown*, 21.

2. Pippa Norris, Sarah Cameron, and Thomas Wynter, eds., *Electoral Integrity in America: Securing Democracy* (New York: Oxford University Press, 2019), 35.

3. Kris W. Kobach, "Exclusive—Kobach: It Appears Out-of-State Voters Changed Outcome of New Hampshire U.S. Senate Race," www.breitbart.com /politics/2017/09/07/exclusive-kobach-out-of-state-voters-changed-outcome -new-hampshire-senate-race/.

4. Ben Kamisar, "Kobach Defends Controversial Breitbart Column on NH Voter Fraud," *The Hill*, September 12, 2017, https://thehill.com/home news/administration/350270-kobach-defends-controversial-breitbart -column-on-nh-voter-fraud.

5. Levitsky and Ziblatt, *How Democracies Die*, 186.

6. John Wagner, "Trump Voting Fraud Panel Member Lamented Adding Democrats, 'Mainstream' Republicans," *Washington Post*, September 13, 2017, www.washingtonpost.com/politics/trump-voting-panel-member-lamented -inclusion-of-democrats-mainstream-republicans/2017/09/13/03f89a90-98bb -11e7-82e4-f1076f6d6152_story.html.

7. Norris, Cameron, and Wynter, *Electoral Integrity in America*, 35.

8. Mark Crispin Miller, *Fooled Again: How the Right Stole the 2004 Election and Why They'll Steal the Next One Too (Unless We Stop Them)* (New York: Basic Books, 2005), 27.

9. John Conyers and Gore Vidal, *What Went Wrong in Ohio: The Conyers Report on the 2004 Presidential Election*, ed. Anita Miller (Chicago: Academy Chicago Publishers, 2005), x.

10. Quoted in Hasen, *Election Meltdown*, 31.

11. Brooke Seipel, "Mississippi Official: Fraud Commission Can 'Go Jump in Gulf of Mexico,'" *The Hill*, June 30, 2017, https://thehill.com/blogs/blog-briefing -room/news/340307-miss-official-on-trump-voter-fraud-request-they-can-go -jump-in.

12. "*Fish v. Kobach*—Findings of Fact and Conclusions of Law," American Civil Liberties Union, www.aclu.org/legal-document/fish-v-kobach-findings-fact-and -conclusions-law, 3.

Chapter 10: *The System Cannot Protect Itself*

1. There are actually six certified copies. In addition to the one sent to Vice President Pence, two will be sent to the archivist of the United States, two will be sent to Pennsylvania's secretary of state, and one to the chief judge of the local federal district court.

Chapter 11: *The Electoral College Revisited, Alas*

1. I asked Justice Ginsburg this question during her visit to Amherst College on October 3, 2019.
2. Sanford Levinson and Jack M. Balkin, *Democracy and Dysfunction* (Chicago and London: University of Chicago Press, 2019), 33.
3. Steven Shepard, "Poll: Voters Prefer Popular Vote over Electoral College," *Politico*, March 27, 2019, https://politi.co/2FzbV2t.
4. Issacharoff, *Fragile Democracies*, 24.
5. The 2004 election represented a very near miss; had John Kerry won Ohio, where electoral irregularities were rampant, he would have won the electoral vote despite losing the national popular vote to Bush.
6. Michael Geruso, Dean Spears, and Ishaana Talesara, "Inversions in US Presidential Elections: 1836–2016," University of Texas Electoral College Study, September 6, 2019, http://utecs.org/wp-content/uploads/NBERWP.pdf. The research found a 32 percent chance of "electoral inversion" in a race decided by less than 2 percent of votes cast; a 45 percent chance in a race decided by less than 1 percent; and a 77 percent chance that the electoral inversion will favor the Republican candidate.
7. Robert S. McElvaine, "HNN Poll: How Historians Rank the Presidency of George W. Bush (2008)," History News Network, http://hnn.us/articles/47918.html. See also the harsh assessment of Jean Edward Smith, *Bush* (New York: Simon & Schuster, reprint, 2017).
8. Issacharoff, *Fragile Democracies*, 34.
9. Quoted in Mark Chou, "Sowing the Seeds of Its Own Destruction: Democracy and Democide in the Weimar Republic and Beyond," *Theoria: A Journal of Social and Political Theory* 59, no. 133 (2012): 21–49, at 22.
10. See generally Benjamin Carter Hett, *The Death of Democracy: Hitler's Rise to Power and the Downfall of the Weimar Republic* (New York: Henry Holt, 2018).
11. Donald S. Lutz, "Toward a Theory of Constitutional Amendment," *American Political Science Review* 88, no. 2 (1994): 355. Lutz finds the U.S. Constitution the second most difficult to amend. Some scholars give this distinction to the Canadian constitution.
12. Maine's district system went into effect in 1972, Nebraska's in 1992.
13. Christopher Ingraham, "How Doug Jones Lost in Nearly Every Congressional District but Still Won the State," *Washington Post*, December 13, 2017, www.washingtonpost.com/news/wonk/wp/2017/12/13/how-doug-jones-lost-in-nearly-every-congressional-district-but-still-won-the-state/.
14. In *Rucho v. Common Cause*, the Supreme Court's conservative majority recently

acknowledged that gerrymandering "leads to results that reasonably seem unjust" but declared the Court incapable of shaping a remedy, a painful punt that reminds us that awarding electoral votes on a districtwide basis promises only to make our presidential elections turn on a radically antidemocratic fixture of our present political reality. *Rucho v. Common Cause*, No. 18-422 588 U.S. ___ (2019). Argued March 26, 2019—decided June 27, 2019, 30.

15. Some experts insist that the Constitution does not delegate to states the power to effectively amend our system of electing the president. See, for example, "Some experts insist that the Constitution does not delegate," Independence Institute, February 4, 2019, https://i2i.org/why-the-national-public-vote-scheme -is-unconstitutional/. Indeed, it seems likely that the Supreme Court would deem the NPVIC scheme the kind of "Agreement or Compact" that, by the lights of Article I, §10 of the Constitution, would require the "Consent of Congress," something the scheme could not possibly receive.

16. This is not to say that nothing can be done to stop an NPVIC state from breaking ranks. Having passed a law pledging the state's electoral votes to the national popular vote winner, a state legislature cannot simply decide to essentially change its election law *after* the election to alter a result that it doesn't like. Such an act would certainly invite challenges in the courts. In addition, under the terms of the Electoral Count Act of 1887 (see extensive discussion in later chapters), such a change would also deprive the state's Electoral College certificate from "safe harbor" status in Congress. This would authorize Congress to disqualify the state's electoral votes, which, as we shall see, raises exceptionally fraught legal and political questions.

17. Unless combined with some other device, such as an instant runoff, the NPVIC would also be vulnerable to this countermajoritarian outcome. See extensive discussion in Edward B. Foley, *Presidential Elections and Majority Rule: The Rise, Demise, and Potential Restoration of the Jeffersonian Electoral College* (New York: Oxford University Press, 2020).

Chapter 12: *A Constitutional Anachronism*

1. See Akhil Amar and Vikram Amar, "History, Slavery, Sexism, the South, and the Electoral College," FindLaw, November 30, 2001, https://supreme.findlaw .com/legal-commentary/history-slavery-sexism-the-south-and-the-electoral -college.html.

2. Michael J. Glennon, *When No Majority Rules: The Electoral College and Presidential Succession* (Washington, DC: Congressional Quarterly, 1992), 7.

3. Quoted in Matthew J. Streb, *Rethinking American Electoral Democracy*, 3rd ed. (Controversies in Electoral Democracy and Representation) (New York: Routledge, 2016), 162.

4. *Federalist* No. 68, available at www.congress.gov/resources/display/content /The+Federalist+Papers#TheFederalistPapers-68.

5. Gary L. Rose, ed., *Controversial Issues in Presidential Selection*, 2nd ed. (Albany: SUNY Press, 1994), 201.

6. Article II, Section 1, available at "The Constitution of the United States: A Transcription," National Archives, November 4, 2015, https://www.archives.gov/founding-docs/constitution-transcript.

7. Foley, *Presidential Elections and Majority Rule*, 50.

8. After their admission as states, Florida and Colorado also briefly relied on the system of legislative appointment. At present, three-quarters of the states authorize parties to stage state conventions where they nominate their electors. Several other states, including the District of Columbia, permit state party committees to nominate their electors.

9. Quoted in Glennon, *When No Majority Rules*, 13.

10. *Ray v. Blair*, 343 U.S. 214 (1952), available at Library of Congress, www.loc.gov/item/usrep343214/.

Chapter 13: *Catastrophe No. 1*

1. Quoted in Lawrence D. Longley and Neal R. Peirce, *The Electoral College Primer* (New Haven, CT: Yale University Press, 1996), 105.

2. Quoted in Longley and Peirce, *Electoral College Primer*, 103.

3. "Faithless Elector State Laws," FairVote, www.fairvote.org/faithless_elector_state_laws.

4. *Baca v. Colorado Department of State*, No. 18-1173 (10th Cir. 2019), available at Justia Law, https://law.justia.com/cases/federal/appellate-courts/ca10/18-1173/18-1173-2019-08-20.html.

5. *Baca v. Colorado*, 113, 2, 90.

6. *In the Matter of Levi Guerra, Esther John, and Peter Chiafalo*, Supreme Court of the State of Washington, No. 95347-3 (May 23, 2019).

7. In 1892, the Supreme Court recognized the plenary power of states to decide how electors are chosen but not whether that power extended to how electors actually voted. *McPherson v. Blacker*, 146 U.S. 1 (1892).

8. *Ray v. Blair*, 343 U.S. 214 (1952).

9. *Ray v. Blair*, 343 U.S. 214 (1952). The case was decided 5–2, with Hugo Black and Felix Frankfurter not participating, 232.

10. Paul Smith, "This Court Case Could Bring Chaos to the Electoral College," *Talking Points Memo*, October 4, 2019, https://talkingpointsmemo.com/cafe/electoral-college-court-cases.

11. Levinson and Balkin, *Democracy and Dysfunction*, 91–92.

12. Jack Maskell and Elizabeth Rybicki, "Counting Electoral Votes: An Overview of Procedures at the Joint Session, Including Objections by Members of Congress," n.d., Congressional Research Service, November 15, 2016, https://fas.org/sgp/crs/misc/RL32717.pdf, 4.

13. See generally Michael F. Holt, *By One Vote: The Disputed Presidential Election of 1876* (Lawrence: University Press of Kansas, 2008).

14. Foley, *Ballot Battles*, 119.

15. Nathan L. Colvin and Edward B. Foley, "The Twelfth Amendment: A

Constitutional Ticking Time Bomb," *University of Miami Law Review* 64, no. 2 (2010): 475–534.

16. Story quoted in United States Congress, *Counting Electoral Votes: Proceedings and Debates of Congress Relating to Counting the Electoral Votes for President and Vice-President of the United States* (Washington, DC: Government Printing Office, 1877).

17. United States Congress, *Counting Electoral Votes: Proceedings and Debates of Congress Relating to Counting the Electoral Votes for President and Vice-President of the United States* (U.S. Government Printing Office, 1877), vii.

18. Longley and Peirce, *Electoral College Primer*, 28.

19. George C. Edwards III, *Why the Electoral College Is Bad for America* (New Haven, CT: Yale University Press, 2005), 47.

20. Foley, *Ballot Battles*, 132.

21. The Twentieth Amendment, adopted in 1933, pushed inauguration day forward to January 20, and while there is nothing magical about these dates, they are fixed by the Constitution and so allow no wiggle room.

22. Codified as 3 U.S. Code §§ 5–6, 15–18 (2006).

23. Foley, *Ballot Battles*, 157.

24. Foley, *Ballot Battles*, 355.

25. Colvin and Foley, "Twelfth Amendment," 477.

26. Stephen A. Siegel, "The Conscientious Congressman's Guide to the Electoral Count Act of 1887," *Florida Law Review* 56 (2010), 544.

27. Congress had, in the distant past, rejected state electoral votes. In 1865, Congress voted to exclude the votes of southern states, even those, such as Louisiana and Tennessee, that had already been returned to Union control. In 1869 and in 1873—that is, during Reconstruction—Congress again rejected votes from southern states. (Recall that while the elections occurred in November 1868 and November 1872, Congress did not review the count until the following January.) In 1873, Congress rejected Arkansas' electoral certificate because it lacked a state seal, notwithstanding the fact that Arkansas did not have a state seal. But no vote had been rejected since the adoption of the ECA. Colvin and Foley, "Twelfth Amendment," 498.

28. 3 U.S. Code § 15. Counting Electoral Votes in Congress. Available at Legal Information Institute, Cornell Law School, www.law.cornell.edu/uscode/text/3/15.

29. Colvin and Foley, "Twelfth Amendment," 521.

30. 3 U.S. Code § 15. Counting Electoral Votes in Congress.

31. 3 U.S. Code § 19. Vacancy in Offices of Both President and Vice President; Officers Eligible to Act. Available at Legal Information Institute, Cornell Law School, www.law.cornell.edu/uscode/text/3/19.

Chapter 14: *Catastrophe No. 2*

1. I am grateful to Rick Hasen for first suggesting this scenario. See also Hasen, *Election Meltdown*.

2. "Michigan Presidential Race Results: Donald J. Trump Wins," *New York Times*,

August 1, 2017, www.nytimes.com/elections/2016/results/michigan-president
-clinton-trump.

3. Michael Wines, "$250 Million to Keep Votes Safe? Experts Say Billions Are Needed," *New York Times*, September 25, 2019, www.nytimes.com/2019/09/25 /us/mitch-mcconnell-election-security-bill-.html.

4. Levitsky and Ziblatt, *How Democracies Die*, 61.

5. Jamin Raskin quoted in Streb, *Rethinking American Electoral Democracy*, 166.

6. Hasen, *Election Meltdown*, 51.

7. "Help America Vote Act | U.S. Election Assistance Commission," accessed January 27, 2020, www.eac.gov/about/help-america-vote-act.

8. David E. Sanger and Catie Edmondson, "Russia Targeted Election Systems in All 50 States, Report Finds," *New York Times*, July 25, 2019, www.nytimes .com/2019/07/25/us/politics/russian-hacking-elections.html.

9. Hasen, *Election Meltdown*, 91–92.

10. Rubio quoted in Hasen, *Election Meltdown*, 92.

11. 116th Congress, 1st Session, Senate, *Report of the Select Committee on Intelligence United States Senate on Russian Active Measures Campaigns and Interference in the 2016 U.S. Election*, vol. 1, *Russian Efforts Against Election Infrastructure with Additional Views*, 35, www.intelligence.senate.gov/sites/default/files/documents /Report_Volume1.pdf.

12. "What Does Election Security Cost?," Brennan Center for Justice, accessed December 16, 2019, www.brennancenter.org/our-work/analysis-opinion/what -does-election-security-cost.

13. Thomas Nilsen, "Norwegian Votes to Be Counted Manually in Fear of Election Hacking," *Barents Observer*, September 11, 2017, https://thebarentsobserver .com/en/life-and-public/2017/09/norwegian-votes-be-counted-manually-fear -election-hacking.

14. Sanger and Edmondson, "Russia Targeted Election Systems in All 50 States, Report Finds."

15. Wines, "$250 Million to Keep Votes Safe?"

16. Sanger and Edmondson, "Russia Targeted Election Systems in All 50 States, Report Finds."

17. Hasen, *Election Meltdown*, 63.

18. "A Look at the Vulnerabilities and Capabilities of American Cybersecurity," *All Things Considered*, NPR, July 16, 2019, www.npr.org/2019/07/16/742386872 /a-look-at-the-vulnerabilities-and-capabilities-of-american-cybersecurity, transcript, 5.

19. Hasen, *Election Meltdown*, 94.

20. "Russian Government Cyber Activity Targeting Energy and Other Critical Infrastructure Sectors," Cybersecurity and Infrastructure Security Agency, www.us-cert.gov/ncas/alerts/TA18-074A.

21. "Election Emergencies Happen," *The Canvass: States and Election Reform*,

National Conference of State Legislatures, August 2008, www.ncsl.org/research /elections-and-campaigns/election-emergencies-happen.aspx.

22. Quoted in Hasen, *Election Meltdown*, 95.

23. Matt Vasilogambros, "When Elections Get a Do-Over," Pew, December 26, 2018, https://pew.org/2Bzj9Sl.

From the article:

"In Indiana, the state Supreme Court in 2004 ordered a new mayoral contest in East Chicago after alleged absentee ballot fraud.

"And in Connecticut, the Supreme Court in 2006 ordered a new Middletown city council election because of errors by officials.

"One of the most high-profile do-overs happened after the 1974 federal election, when two recounts and a U.S. Senate review couldn't determine a winner to fill a New Hampshire U.S. Senate seat. Democrat John Durkin eventually won the seat in a new election in September 1975 by 27,000 votes."

24. 3 U.S. Code § 2. Failure to Make Choice on Prescribed Day. Available at Legal Information Institute, Cornell Law School, www.law.cornell.edu/uscode/text/3/2.

25. See *Donohue v. Board of Elections of State of NY*, 435 F. Supp. 957 (E.D.N.Y. 1976), available at Justia Law, https://law.justia.com/cases/federal/district -courts/FSupp/435/957/1424690/. There, a federal court held that for a court to issue such an extraordinary remedy based on a § 1983 claim or directly based on a Fourteenth Amendment claim, the election fraud or unlawful behavior must be committed by persons acting under color of state law or by private persons acting jointly with state officials.

26. 3 U.S. Code § 5. Determination of Controversy as to Appointment of Electors. Available at Legal Information Institute, Cornell Law School, www.law.cornell .edu/uscode/text/3/5.

27. The election of 1856 witnessed something analogous. A massive snowstorm in Wisconsin prevented the state's electors from casting their votes on the required date. Congress had never anticipated or dealt with the issue, and for two days debate raged over whether the belated electoral certificate should be counted. The president of the Senate chose to accept Wisconsin's vote, though the controversy remained unsettled. This occurred, we should recall, before the passage of the ECA. Colvin and Foley, "Twelfth Amendment," 495.

28. 3 U.S. Code §15. Counting Electoral Votes in Congress. Available at Legal Information Institute, Cornell Law School, www.law.cornell.edu/uscode/text/3/15.

29. Michael Stern, "How to Count to 270: The Electoral Count Act and the Election of 2000," *Point of Order*, January 14, 2016, www.pointoforder.com/2016/01 /14/how-to-count-to-270-the-electoral-count-act-and-the-election-of-2000/. See Vasan Kesavan, "Is the Electoral Count Act Unconstitutional?," *North Carolina Law Review* 80, no. 5 (2002): 1653–1813, at 1695 and 1784, available at https://doi.org/10.2139/ssrn.371480.

30. Colvin and Foley, "Twelfth Amendment," 526.

Chapter 15: *Catastrophe No. 3*

1. "EAVS Deep Dive: Absentee and Mail Voting," U.S. Election Assistance Commission, October 17, 2017, www.eac.gov/documents/2017/10/17/eavs-deep-dive-early-absentee-and-mail-voting-data-statutory-overview/. "A 2016 Survey of the Performance of American Elections (SPAE) found that 33 percent of voters 70 years and older voted absentee, compared to 20 percent of voters in their thirties."

2. Matthew Haag, "Mitch McConnell Calls Push to Make Election Day a Holiday a Democratic 'Power Grab,'" *New York Times*, January 31, 2019, www.nytimes.com/2019/01/31/us/politics/election-day-holiday-mcconnell.html.

3. Jonathan Lai, "Pa.'s Absentee-Ballot Problem: Votes Come in Late Because of Tight Deadlines," *Philadelphia Inquirer*, August 8, 2018, www.inquirer.com/philly/news/politics/pennsylvania-absentee-ballot-voting-deadline-missed-uncounted-20180808.html.

4. "Data 'Deep Dive' Examines Provisional Voting Trends Nationwide," U.S. Election Assistance Commission, www.eac.gov/news/2018/06/07/data-deep-dive-examines-provisional-voting-trends-nationwide-election-administration-and-voting-survey-eavs-provisional-voting-ballot-data-media/.

5. The Help America Vote Act requires states to offer provisional ballots. The only exceptions are states that offered same-day voter registration in 1993 when the National Voter Registration Act became law—Idaho, Minnesota, New Hampshire, North Dakota, Wisconsin, and Wyoming. Idaho, Minnesota, and New Hampshire do not provide for provisional voting. North Dakota provides for provisional balloting only in the event of a court order extending polling hours.

6. "Provisional Ballots," MIT Election Data + Science Lab, https://electionlab.mit.edu/research/provisional-ballots. It is worth noting that the rejection rate ran higher in presidential election years than in midterms, with 79 percent of provisional ballots issued being counted.

7. Provisional ballots submitted in the wrong jurisdiction or precinct accounted for 18 percent of rejections nationwide. "Data 'Deep Dive' Examines Provisional Voting Trends Nationwide," U.S. Election Assistance Commission.

8. Edward B. Foley, "Preparing for a Disputed Presidential Election: An Exercise in Election Risk Assessment and Management," *Loyola University Chicago Law Journal*, forthcoming, available at https://papers.ssrn.com/abstract=3446021.

9. Foley, "Preparing for a Disputed Presidential Election," 3.

10. Joshua Jamerson, Alex Leary, and Andrew Duehren, "Republican Rick Scott Wins Senate Race in Florida," *Wall Street Journal*, November 19, 2018, www.wsj.com/articles/florida-senate-race-set-to-come-to-a-close-as-recount-wraps-up-1542538800.

11. German Lopez, "The Florida Voter Fraud Allegations, Explained," *Vox*, November 12, 2018, www.vox.com/policy-and-politics/2018/11/12/18084786/florida-midterm-elections-senate-governor-results-fraud.

12. Donald J. Trump, tweet, November 12, 2018, https://twitter.com/realdonald trump/status/1061962869376540672?lang=en.
13. Hasen, *Election Meltdown*, 107.
14. Quoted in Hasen, *Election Meltdown*, 108.
15. Miller, *Fooled Again*, 91–92.
16. Miller, *Fooled Again*, 90.
17. Foley, "Preparing for a Disputed Presidential Election," 6.
18. It should be noted that the Court's decision—to halt the recount rather than let Florida lose its safe harbor protection—has been roundly criticized by leading constitutionalists. See Laurence H. Tribe, "*Erog v. Hsub* and its Disguises: Freeing *Bush v. Gore* from its Hall of Mirrors," 115 *Harvard Law Review* 170 (2001), https://papers.ssrn.com/sol3/papers.cfm?abstract_id=433960.
19. Nixon quoted in Colvin and Foley, "The Twelfth Amendment," 520.

Chapter 16: *Can the Crisis Be Contained?*

1. Jose A. DelReal, "Donald Trump Accuses Ted Cruz of Fraud in Iowa Caucuses, Calls for Results to Be Invalidated," *Washington Post*, February 3, 2016, www.washingtonpost.com/news/post-politics/wp/2016/02/03/donald-trump -accuses-ted-cruz-of-fraud-in-iowa-caucuses-calls-for-results-to-be-invalidated/.
2. Such an act has precedent. John Quincy Adams boycotted Andrew Jackson's inauguration, as did Andrew Johnson Ulysses S. Grant's.
3. Bernard Gwertzman, "Pentagon Kept Tight Rein in Last Days of Nixon Rule," *New York Times*, August 25, 1974, www.nytimes.com/1974/08/25/archives /pentagon-kept-tight-reinin-last-days-of-nixon-rule-no-event.html.
4. The election of 1884 turned on the result in New York State, where Grover Cleveland defeated James Blaine by 1,047 votes. The election of 1888 has been called the most corrupt in U.S. history. Election expert Ned Foley has described the fact that none of these elections devolved into an 1876-like mess as "something of a miracle." Foley, *Ballot Battles*, 150.

Chapter 17: *Republicans Reject Democracy*

1. Levitsky and Ziblatt, *How Democracies Die*, 136.
2. Levitsky and Ziblatt, *How Democracies Die*, 166.
3. Levitsky and Ziblatt, *How Democracies Die*, 135, 163.
4. Benjamin Rhodes, *The World as It Is: A Memoir of the Obama White House* (New York: Random House, 2018), 394.
5. "McConnell Threatened Brennan & Obama to Prevent CIA Disclosure of Putin's 2016 Interference," *Daily Kos*, October 2, 2018, www.dailykos.com/story/2018 /10/2/1800802/-McConnell-threatened-Brennan-amp-Obama-to-prevent -CIA-disclosure-of-Putin-s-2016-interference.
6. Or consider Pennsylvania GOP congressman Guy Reschenthaler's response to the Mueller report documenting Russian interference in the 2016 election. The

report, Reschenthaler tweeted, "flies in the face of American justice" and was nothing short of "un-American." Rep. Guy Reschenthaler, tweet, July 24, 2019, https://twitter.com/GReschenthaler/status/1154074535056084993.

7. Yascha Mounk, *The People vs. Democracy: Why Our Freedom Is in Danger and How to Save It* (Cambridge, MA: Harvard University Press, 2018), 118.

8. Mitch Smith, "Fears of Republican Power Grab in Michigan Fade as Governor Vetoes Bill," *New York Times*, December 28, 2018, www.nytimes.com /2018/12/28/us/michigan-snyder-power-veto.html.

9. Julie Turkewitz, "Oregon Climate Walkout Left Republicans in Hiding, Statehouse in Disarray," *New York Times*, June 28, 2019, www.nytimes.com/2019/06/28/us /oregon-climate-fight.html.

10. Mounk, *The People vs. Democracy*, 116.

11. Mounk, *The People vs. Democracy*, 261.

Chapter 18: *The Only Check*

1. Issacharoff, *Fragile Democracies*, 205.

2. Issacharoff, *Fragile Democracies*, 205.

3. Issacharoff, *Fragile Democracies*, 206.

4. Foley, *Ballot Battles*, 355.

INDEX

election of 2020 (*Cont.*)

    constitutional crisis projected for, 5, 55, 78

    crisis scenario #1: faithless electors lead to Pelosi named acting president, 62–64, 66–67, 70–79

    crisis scenario #2: hack of Michigan voting machines and Trump loses on revote, 81–92

    crisis scenario #3: Democratic candidate wins by narrow margin after counting of absentee, provisional ballots, 3–5, 45, 93–103

    Democrats' goal of removing Trump, ix–x

    election day (Nov. 3), 43, 45

    justification for constitutional usurpation, 37

    Trump and foreign interference, 18

    Trump loses the popular vote, 50, 54, 105

    Trump loses without conceding defeat, 105–7

    Trump protecting his brand and, 27, 29, 78, 106

    Trump rejecting defeat, x, 3–5, 7–9, 27–28, 43, 77–79, 103, 105–9

    Trump's campaign finances, 5

    Trump's likelihood of winning, 5, 105, 118

    Trump's own words in 2016 and, 7–9

election of 2024

    chances of a Trump candidacy, 108

    statute of limitations on Trump indictment and, 25

Electoral College, 37, 49–55

    abolishing, 115

    capacity to misfire, 49–50, 51, 109, 126n5

    certificates rejected by Congress, instances of, 129n27

    as a constitutional anachronism, 57–60

    contested elections and, 54–55, 67–70, 73, 78, 89, 102, 109, 133n4

    contradictory certificates sent to Congress, 67, 68–69, 78, 90–91, 100–101, 102, 109

    critics of, 49, 60

    date of voting in, 2020 (Dec. 14), 43, 44, 62, 89

    defenders of, 54

    delayed certificate validity, 131n27

    district plan for, 52, 126n12

    election of 1800, 44, 55, 63, 109

    election of 1824, 44, 63

    election of 1876, 55, 67–70, 78, 109

    election of 2000, 55, 61, 109

    election of 2016, Trump wins Electoral College, loses popular vote, 5, 11

    election of 2020, crisis scenario #1, faithless electors vote against Trump, 62–64, 70–79

    election of 2020, Trump's likelihood of winning the Electoral College, losing popular vote, 54

    "electoral inversion" and, 126n6

    faithless elector laws in states, 64–65

    faithless electors, 61–62, 64, 71–72, 109

    framers and creation of, 58–59, 68

    how it works, 43–44

    how states award electoral votes, 52, 59

    how states choose electors, 59, 127–28n8, 128n7

    Jackson on electors, 59

    Maine's electors, 2016, 52

    NPVIC initiative and, 52–53, 127n16, 127n17

    as opaque system, 51

    Pennsylvania's votes in, 44

    popular vote vs., 49–50

    results mailed to the president of the Senate on Jan. 6, 44, 66–68, 125–26n1

    swing states and, 85

    voter machine vulnerability and, 83, 85

ABOUT THE AUTHOR

Lawrence Douglas is the James J. Grosfeld Professor of Law, Jurisprudence and Social Thought at Amherst College. A graduate of Brown and Yale Law School, Professor Douglas has received numerous honors, including major fellowships from the National Endowment for the Humanities, the American Council of Learned Societies, and the Carnegie Foundation. He is the author of six previous books, including the widely acclaimed *The Memory of Judgment: Making Law and History in the Trials of the Holocaust* and *The Right Wrong Man: John Demjanjuk and the Last Great Nazi War Crimes Trial*, a *New York Times* "Editor's Choice." His novel *The Vices* was a finalist for the National Jewish Book Prize. His work has appeared in numerous publications, including *Harper's*, the *New York Times*, the *New Yorker* and the *Los Angeles Times*. He is a regular contributor to the *Times Literary Supplement* and the *Guardian*, where, since 2016, he has been writing about legal issues involving the Trump presidency.